100 Ideas To Build Stronger Families

100 Ideas To Build Stronger Families

Jeffrey L. Slack

2009

Contents

INTRODUCTION

There is an interesting shift occurring right now that on one hand some social scientists are stating family values are under attack; on the other hand, historians and some other social scientists state that family has been the foundation of all that is important or good. Either way you view it, family has always been important and we need to be alert to keep family values and building opportunities at the forefront of all we do.

Because of the nature of many of our lives, this isn't always easy. Busy schedules, ever-changing technology, youth sports, increased homework requirements, career ambitions and maintenance of our stuff all seem to take precedence over our family time. This in addition to compromising on items the entire family can enjoy, make increased family time a tough sell for many families. Sometimes we need help in finding ways to keep connectivity open no matter what the situation is in our respective families.

100 Ideas To Build Stronger Families is a project that was birthed out of an understanding of these needs invading our family and a desire to help families find more ways to bond. It was written with an understanding of the pressures and roadblocks that families face in trying to come up with ideas to draw their families close. Not all the ideas will be useful for you in your particular family's situation and personality, but some of them might click as being possibilities. Some of them might just be affirmations that what you are currently doing is good and needs to be continued. Either way, we hope these ideas are helpful.

As you look through the book, try to keep an open mind when these ideas might have an opportunity to be used. Talk over these different possibilities with your spouse and children to see

1

if any of these ideas peak their interest; allow these ideas to initiate some dialogue on what are some ways the family can spend time together and be drawn together in the process. Have fun with these ideas, they are meant for your family's enjoyment and bonding.

As far as the stories and illustrations, they are all true. I have opened a window into the soul of our family to allow you to view what we are all about. I believe I have a pretty amazing family, but we work hard at it. I wouldn't be the man I am today without their help. My prayer for you and your family is that you will be able to experience the closeness and unity that we experience regularly in our home.

1

Go To Sporting Events Together

My family loves to go to sporting events; not because we are sports nuts, but because it's a fun day (or night) together. The fans, the food, the intense action; there is nothing quite the same as enjoying the atmosphere around a game. Whatever your local team and whatever your sport of choice, it can be a time of great family fun to sit next to each other and cheer for victory.

Going to a game doesn't have to be relegated to the seats to have fun also. Tailgating is a great way before the game to draw your family (and others, also) closer together. Barbequing, playing catch, talking about great games you saw as a child; these are good things to share with your kids. Food can also be brought premade and shared like a picnic. Most stadiums are open to tailgaters but check beforehand to verify.

Once inside the stadium, the mood changes and it's time to get into the game. If you are a fan, make sure to wear your team colors to show your spirit. This is also a great place to talk about team players who are good role models. Kids still need heroes and many sports figures do a great job recognizing they are on display and do their best to portray a positive lifestyle.

If your children are young, make sure to dress them appropriately for the weather. If a game is being played at night, bring a blanket and warm jackets, because kids will notoriously get cold and tired. And always remember, no matter how diehard of a fan you are; your kids are watching and you need to model your speech and behavior (which includes drinking alcohol) because you want to convey a positive message about your time at the stadium; this is about family time more then supporting the team.

P.S. My family gets great seats on Stubhub and Ebay regularly for amazing prices; why pay full retail?

2

Attend Children's Sporting Events Regularly

Let's face it, life is short. Your time with your kids: even shorter. Time watching them play sports: just a blip compared to everything else. But as far as impact on your child's life, it's huge. Kids practice hard, they are trying hard to learn the game and they also want to show you (their number one fan) how much they have improved. But life is busy and there are many choices you have to make to decide what will take precedence.

Your kids deserve a place in your life that takes precedence over many other aspects in your life; that's just the way it should be. If you want a tight family, you need to make it a priority to get to your kids practices and games. These kids are depending on you (their number one fan) to be there cheering them on when they score that goal, catch that touchdown or slide safely into home. Some of my best memories with my kids have been watching them excel at a sport they have worked hard at and watching them when they make that play and then looking over to the stands or sidelines (and they always look!) to make sure we caught that moment.

Now exceptions do happen and I have had my share of them. But because of the sensitivity of this area with my kids; we always discuss when I can't make it because of another engagement that I have no control over changing. They know I am usually at the practices and games and when I can't make it; it's because it's out of my control. But I make it when possible and hate it when I miss. If I do miss I make sure to call my kids before the game to let them know I am thinking of them and I call them afterwards to see how it went. This is a huge part of their life and when it becomes a huge part of your life also it will serve as a bonding time for your family.

P.S. This last year I had the rare blessing of seeing both of my kids play in championship games for soccer and baseball; I wouldn't trade those moments for any job performance review in the world.

3

Eat dinner together at least five nights per week

For my family, eating dinner together is the norm, not the exception. Growing up for me this wasn't such a big deal, which made it harder for it to become a discipline. Studies have shown that families that eat dinner together regularly are more apt to be closer; which for my wife and I was our goal that we set before we started having children.

Soccer practice, school assignments, guitar lessons, orthodontist visits and grocery shopping are just some of the daily challenges that cause our schedule to border on the side of chaotic. These things are all good to have in our schedule, but dinner together is one of those few times in life when we sit down together and enjoy a meal and have a family conversation. This time needs to not only be protected, but also encouraged within the family. If a goal to eat together at dinnertime is not guarded from outside and even inside influences; it's very easy for everyone to eat when they want and not ever have to interact with others from the family.

For two weeks monitor your family dinnertimes and determine whether or not your family eats dinner together at least

3-4 nights per week. Begin to alter your family's schedules to protect that dinnertime slot and move your family toward eating together 5 nights per week. Make sure to take advantage of the time and discuss the day and what is going on in each person's life. This is also a good time to talk through good family business and upcoming plans (save any disciplinary discussions for another time). Make sure not to have silent dinners and instead strive for healthy, positive dialogues.

P.S. One of our favorite dinners to eat together is my wife's homemade macaroni and cheese. This dish is too die for and my family leaves no leftovers when my wife blesses us with this great meal.

4

Take Walks Together

Walking is great exercise; good for the heart, the lungs, the back and the legs. It's also a great way to spend family time together. Whether walking around a park, on a walking trail, or around the block; it's a completely positive way to share some time.

Walking together is also a way to model for your kids what a healthy lifestyle entails. Your children are shaping their minds now for what their own lives will look like later; When they see exercise modeled as a regular part of life, they will be more inclined to develop healthy habits as they get older.

Sometimes kids might not want to walk at an adults pace or even an adult distance; It's okay to let kids ride bikes, scooters, skateboards or skates during this time. The message is still the same: healthy people get out and work at staying fit; they know it doesn't happen on a couch playing a video game or watching the TV.

But let's face it, it might not be your kids we have to worry about here; you need to get out there and do some exercising. Start small and as you conquer one small walk, add a little to that. Keep slowly adding until you reach your goal. If walking outside doesn't work for you; go to the mall and walk around inside; while you look for that new outfit you'll need after you shed all those lbs.

P.S. Our family lives in the Inland Empire area of California; sometimes at night when walking, the aroma of cows is wafting through the area.

5

Plan a vacation together and go on it

Most families when planning a vacation, go where the adults want to go and don't give the children the opportunity to input (hey, the adults are paying, right?). But how much cooler would that vacation be to the family if the children had the opportunity to participate in the decision making process and help decide where the family was headed. Now, this might get pigeonholed and expensive (Can you say Disneyland and the Disneyland Hotel, over and over again); but it doesn't have to go in that direction.

Give children options that you are looking at and let them help choose one of them. Let them help research each possibility and give them the budget that you are working within. Let them look for things to do in the destination area that keep the family within the budget. Give each child the opportunity to plan a day or outing while on the vacation. Be patient with your children as they explore what living within boundaries can look like. Get together a list of all the items that need to happen and be collected before your family leaves for the trip.

This gives your children a chance to take part ownership of a big family event. This also helps them see what living within a budget looks like; even for fun things in life. As years go on, your children will remember the vacation, not because they went somewhere different, but because they had an integral part of making it happen.

P.S. Our last big family vacation was to Seattle, Wa. where we spent great family moments at the Space Needle, a tour of Safeco Field and lots of time in the swimming pool.

6

Have a favorite restaurant that you go to once per year

We as a family don't have a problem going out to eat. Whether it's Marie Calendar's with their great salad bar or Black Angus for a nice rib eye; we enjoy eating out. But once in awhile we like to really splurge and go somewhere that is super nice; somewhere that will leave a lasting impression. We found a steak house at the Disneyland Hotel that is a little pricey but my kids are treated like royalty; it definitely leaves my kids wanting to go back. The bonus is there are pictures on the walls of famous celebrities from the fifties, sixties and seventies; this gives us plenty of conversation points as we enjoy the evening.

In this day of over consumerism, why would this be necessary? Because kids need to know first that they are worth the special treatment and second, they need to feel like anything is within their grasp if they work hard enough and save up for the special times.

When we go out once a year to a special restaurant, our kids know we saved for this moment and that this moment is special. We get dressed up, we talk about it for weeks, sometimes, we even get the car valet parked; this adds to the moment.

There are a lot things we spend money on as adults, but our kids need to feel that they are number one. They won't know that unless they see it in your actions as the parents. Why should mom and dad be the only ones to go out to nice dinner; bring the kids and enjoy it as a family.

7

Research your Family Crest and create it as a family art project

This might sound weird, but recently I've become interested in the origins of my family. Not interested in who is married to whom, but rather what are the deep roots of my family and where did we come from. I stumbled upon a website that has done all the research on Family Crests (you know, the symbol on the front of the knight's shield) and I looked up mine and my wife's family and I found both of ours; the bummer is I had to buy the download for the artwork; nothing's free these days. In addition to the crest comes the family history; ours actually seemed believably accurate.

Although I have not yet done the art project with my family, my goal is to work on crests with my family and display them eventually in our family room (makes sense, doesn't it?). My goal would be someday my kids would be fighting over the shields when they are dividing up our huge estate (yea right!)

Why does this have any significance for our family? First, I believe it has significance because it is important for our children to know they are part of a much bigger family; even bigger then the family they see at weddings and funerals. Second, it helps them to see in a very visual picture where they descended from; more so then just telling them they are Italian. Third, it's a really cool discussion piece for my kid's friends when they come over.

My goal is to have actual mini fabricated shields made out of hammered metal and then work out the crest details with my kids. But you can make the shields out of wood (pray for no flaming arrows) or paper or have it made out of quilt material and make a family quilt. The goal is to recognize your family heritage and talk about that while you are creating the project.

8

Take a drive once a month and regularly drive somewhere different and interesting

Living in Southern California, this is not a tough one for us. Driving on PCH, going up to the mountains or going down to San Diego to walk along Fisherman's Wharf; we enjoy driving places together. It's not just the destination we are interested in though; it's the exploring and dialoguing as we go. Some of our favorites places we have found to go, have been on our regular drives.

It's easy for families to get into routines; baseball practice, music lessons, tutoring, video games and channel surfing. Adventure is necessary in families in order to create spontaneous moments of memories.

This becomes important in children because it helps them to have adventurous spirits. If children are constantly forced to live non-spontaneous, regimented lives; it either kills their desire to have go-for-it attitudes or they swing the other way and live out of control because they don't know how to manage the endorphin rush of adventure. Bless your children with a sense of adventure; drive somewhere new and enjoy each other

9

Pray together

There's an old adage that states "Families that pray together, stay together". I really don't know how true that is, except to say, my family is not afraid to pray together and we are really close. This did not happen by accident, my wife and I planned it this way. Even when my children were babies, I would regularly pray out loud for my children's future spouses and that they could be men and women of faith like our kids that were being raised that way. Since our children were born, we have been praying with them and they don't see anything weird about it at all. We pray in public at restaurants, we pray at the dinner table, we pray before we go to sleep, before a big game or when my kids are sick; we pray. As a family of faith it is what we do.

Because we are not afraid to pray, I believe it allows our kids to understand there is nothing to be ashamed of when issues of faith arise. In fact, I believe my kids see us as a bit more in tune with our spirituality because we do know how to pray out loud and we are not afraid of what others think.

Some of the things we pray for are relationships with others, the food we eat, our health, finances, safe travel, helping others and bringing others to church with us. Your family has their own special needs and concerns, but every family I know can benefit in learning how to pray together.

10

Go to church or temple together

Because my wife and I were people of faith before we had kids, my kids have naturally always gone to church with us. The nursery, Sunday School, baptism, Vacation Bible School; plus all the people there, were part of my kids growing up; because I worked as a pastor for many years, there was never any question where we would be on Sunday mornings; at the church. But even though I was employed as a pastor, I never made my kids feel like they were forced to go because we wanted them to always want to go.

For some families, they have never gone to church. I live across the street from a huge ball field. On Sunday mornings when leaving for the church, the park is usually filled with soft-ballers and base-ballers; I wonder if they feel like that is their church. They have community, they teach life lessons, they have communion (donuts and coffee) and they have somewhere to go. But I don't believe it's the same; because the only hope they have is in something temporary and the biggest accomplishment they can shoot for is a scholarship or a tryout with a big league team.

I appreciate the fact that church and the faith lessons that are taught there are something that I am passing off to my kids to hopefully have them pass them off to their kids someday. I also believe that the hope we have in our faith goes beyond the temporary moments of life and extends to the permanent and eternal as well.

11

Learn to play video games together

Although this may sound counter-productive, childish or even a waste of time, I believe playing video games with your children is very beneficial. Our kids actually like it when we enter their world and attempt to learn something from them for a change. Caution must be given though not to make this the time to judge their games that you already gave them permission to purchase (research your kids video game purchases before they buy it). If you don't have the latest and greatest video game system, arcades are still fun and kids still enjoy them like we did.

Why does this activity have real merit though? Because your kids will probably smoke you on any given game (except Asteroids) and it's okay for your kids to see you losing; it shows them on a grander scale that eventually they will probably be smarter, faster and technologically more advanced then their parents (think I'm lying: have you ever tried to teach your parents how to send an email or how to turn on a computer?). This gives kids the chance to be compassionate winners and gain an infant sense of what life will be like someday.

It's also just a great time to hang out together doing something they like to do. It's you putting aside your desires and showing them you value time with them. It's showing them you know you'll probably lose, but that is beside the point anyway. It also gives you a chance to ask them for a change how to do something; kids like feeling empowered and needed. Just think of it as preparing them for that day when they need to decide which nursing home to put you in.

12

Go to college graduations of friends and family together

Both my wife and I highly value education. Although I wasn't raised in a family that thought it was all that important; I learned early on in adulthood that without education, my choices for careers and opportunities would be very limited. As a child, I never went to a college graduation; in fact, my wife's college graduation was the first I had attended. My own high school graduation was the first graduation ceremony I had ever been to; so you get the picture. My wife's family was just the opposite; her parents both had Master's degrees and most of her relatives had college educations. Education was not only important in her family, it was the norm.

Having been in youth ministry all of my own kid's lives, graduations were just part of the package. Students from my jr. high, sr. high and college group would regularly graduate, and we would go to the ceremonies. I even graduated from seminary when my daughter was old enough to attend and remember. What we came to realize is that our kids were seeing hard work come to a place of completion; it gave my own children something to begin to aspire to. We realized attending graduations with our children gave them hope that hard work could pay off.

Whether you have gone to college or not, graduations are a good way to show kids that completion of an academic pursuit is something worth celebrating and something worth pursuing. We can show them diplomas on the wall, we can show them saved assignments that earned an admirable grade, we can even show them what jobs need college educations; but graduations show the celebration and the excitement of a job well done. If it's in May, it's going to be hot; if it's December, it will probably be cold; but they are still worth attending. I believe, the lesson your kids will learn and the discussions you can have just by going cannot be compared to any other lesson on the subject. Do you want your kids to aspire to go to college; take them to some graduations.

13

Cook dinner together once per quarter

Cooking dinner together is different in our family then just eating together. Cooking dinner together is where we all help with something. Because this sometimes can be a bigger challenge then just feeding the kids dinner, we don't do this often. But once in awhile it is a good way to help our kids understand what goes into making a meal and also, how important it is to plan in advance for what you will be making.

Barbequing or making pizza is one of our favorite meals to prepare together. My kids have both spent many moments with me at the barbeque helping to turn the meat while talking about what it takes to grill the perfect rib eye or chicken breast. My daughter and my wife have also spent many hours in the kitchen preparing pizza or enchiladas, of which my 12-year-old daughter is now the expert.

It's no secret that in our society, we are beginning to lose the art of passing down generational recipes and cooking abilities to our children. Microwave dinners and cup o' noodles have become staples for the kitchen cupboard. McDonalds and Taco Bell have become our go-to dinner providers. Local supermarkets offer full-blown holiday dinners for the same price you would pay to make it without the hassle (I won't lie, we've done this).

But at what price are we doing this? Precious family time spent in the kitchen together is being sacrificed.

We as parents need to understand that there is something more precious then our time and convenience, when spending time with our children learning to prepare a meal. Generations before us were doing it and my mom, my mother-in-law and my grandma are/were some of the best cooks I know; and they learned from their parents. Make creating a meal together a special time of investment that will pay off dividends when you are someday invited to their houses. Make creating a meal together an experience of passing on to your children what meal times should be; a time for families to interact with each other.

14

Go to the movies

My family loves going to the movies. Most of the time it is at our local theatre; but because we live in Southern California, occasionally we will splurge and buy premiere tickets to a showing in Hollywood. Movies typically aren't a great way to spend quality time because you need to be quiet; but picking the movie, anticipating the movie and getting to the movie are a great time to dialogue and create some good family moments.

Building up anticipation for the movie is always fun to do together as well. Go online and review the trailers; for most family type movies the websites are typically interactive. Downloading (legally) or buying the soundtrack and listening to the music is also a good way of building up some anticipation.

When we go to the movies, typically there is some kind of meal involved before or after the movie. There is also the trip to the snack bar before the movie begins and there are usually a few video games thrown in just to rid me of any last quarter I might possess. I didn't say it was always cheap; just fun. The key here is to have a good time together. If money is tight; matinees are cheaper. You can also bring in your own candy bars and popcorn as long as you don't broadcast it to the hired help at the theatre. When I was a kid, drive-ins were the cheap way to go; if they still exist in your area; that is always a unique, fun time that kids will remember forever.

15

Talk about the day with each other

With many families, the day goes extremely fast and just getting everything done seems to be the main agenda item. But much can be missed if the chance to debrief about the day's events aren't given any time. This becomes important because children learn that they have the opportunity to gain a perspective that they otherwise might not have had before. It also is important because it teaches kids that you want to dialogue with them and you aren't there just to point out their shortcomings or naïve view of life and relationships.

Almost everyday, I ask my kids how their day went. I want them to know, I'm ready to listen to what they have to say. This easily can be the equivalent of asking coworkers or friends; hey, how are you? Sometimes we want to be polite by asking, but we really don't want to know how they are really doing. Be careful not to do this with your kids, they need you to give them the time they need to unwind.

This is a place also for you to stay current on what is going on in their lives. This seems to be the place that gets many families in trouble; not knowing what is going on; positive or negative. If you daily are dialoguing on what is happening, it's like daily watching the news; you stay fresh on where life is at and there is not too much to surprise you

16

Go on a service project or a mission trip together

It's interesting to note that in the last few years, public and private schools have been recognizing the value of service learning. At almost every level of high school, students are now responsible for completing a certain amount of service type hours through helping organizations or people in need. The reason for this paradigm shift is that academia recognizes that students can learn just as much, if not more from serving others then they can in a classroom. Families can benefit from this lesson in recognizing that much can be learned and also realized when we break away from our typical way of doing life and go beyond our comfort zone to help others.

But beyond just the lesson learned in doing a service project or a mission trip together as a family; a transformation occurs within the value structure of a family. What does your family stand for? Where is your family using their resources and to who's gain? How does your family help others outside of your family circle? These are important questions to wrestle with because as parents, you set the precedent for the values your family will stand for and your kids do watch what you are modeling and there is a good chance they will repeat what you show them. When your children see you and your spouse helping others and sacrificing for their benefit, it creates a dynamic that is unmatched in any other parenting application

For many, thoughts of going on a mission trip or even a service project in the inner-city is a daunting and scary possibility. Let me just say that the old adage "there is nothing to fear, but fear itself" is never truer then in this situation. I can say that I have gone on many mission trips and many service projects and have always come back alive with everyone I've taken (which includes my family and many jr. high and sr. high students). Although caution must always be taken to avoid dangerous and treacherous places, there are many places in the world to go with your family that are safe and people really need your help. If you go to church, check with your pastor, congregational leader, rabbi, etc., and ask if they can recommend a place for you and your family to plug into to offer help. If they can't offer any support you can check with your local rescue mission or Google "Short term Mission Trip" and try to connect with a missions organization doing short-term trips with families (like www.connectthefamily.net).

17

Teach kids how to grocery shop

If you are anything like my wife and I, we believe grocery shopping is better left to the adults; get in and out as quick as possible is the mission. With the added weight (wait?) of kids, grocery shopping can become more of a chore than it already is; hanging on the basket, wanting to get inside the basket, looking for 20 minutes at the cheap toys, getting mad at you for not buying the $9 box of cereal with the coolest toy in it; you know what I'm talking about. We see grocery shopping like we look at cutting the lawn; the quicker I get it done, the less likely somebody is going to get hurt; but is that the best attitude when thinking about our family?

Growing up, I never went to the grocery store with my mom and dad; subsequently, when I got older, I had no clue how to shop. I was a bachelor and I made sure to buy the $9 box of cereal because I didn't know any better (and I neeeeeeeeded that toy!). I bought the things that would appeal to my eyes and my stomach; I shopped based on impulse. This usually meant I wasn't eating as healthy as possible and I was barely able to keep food in the refrigerator long enough between paychecks because I over spent on bare essentials. I had no clue about generic brands, coupons, sale days and planning menus; which would have saved me money each time I went grocery shopping. Until I got married, I was very unwise about smart shopping at the grocery store.

If kids aren't learning how to shop wisely as children, how will they know how to shop when they get older and they are on their own? Much of what they will spend their money on will be impulse decisions. My wife, who does most of the shopping, now takes 1 child with her each time she goes shopping. She doesn't just have them escort her while she is perusing the soda aisle though, she talks to them about why she is choosing one brand over another or when it is okay to choose a generic brand over brand names. She also shows them through discussion and example how coupons save our family money. The grocery store we shop at, shows how much we save each time we utilize coupons and sales; we always make sure to tell our kids so they can understand it makes a difference. This may not seem like that big of a deal now, but repetition trains the mule (or something like that) and the more our kids know about finances, the steps we are taking to maximize our family finances and how they can also benefit from these habits; the better they will understand the value of money. They will be less likely to take family money for granted and they will have a greater respect for what the family has rather then what the family should have.

18

Do something nice for your local police or fire department

Although I believe it is cliché to say that police officers and fire fighters are the unsung heroes of our world; I do believe they deserve as much praise and respect that they do garner. Their job is highly dangerous and I believe we should all feel grateful for the fact that they would be willing to put their lives on the line if it meant doing something to help us. But until a dangerous situation occurs in your family, how often are you letting your children recognize police officers and fire fighters for the great job they are always doing?

I am always blown away during the holiday season when I hear of a family baking cookies or bringing a Thanksgiving meal over to the local police or fire station for the police officers and fire fighters on duty. I think what a great thing to do to honor those men and women who have to be away from their families. But what about the rest of the year? Fire fighting and chasing bad guys is just as dangerous in June as it is in November or December. There are 12 months worth of opportunity to serve these heroes and what a great time of serving and learning as a family as you recognize these men and women of valor.

Baking cookies, bread or a cake; calling the station and telling them you would like to BBQ steaks for them or cook a pot of chili; providing gift cards for a local grocery store (yes, they have to pay for their own meals); having your kids write notes of thanks and encouragement to them; bringing over a couple dozen donuts and coffee; these are all things that you and your family can do together and show your appreciation for the neighborhood heroes. And in addition to the men and women who will appreciate your generosity and care; your children will create a relationship with some heroes that they will never forget. As they grow up they will continue to see their heroes in the community and they will have a deeper appreciation for them. Your children will also come to understand that their family recognizes those in the community that are there to help others.

19

Go camping together

Okay here's the reality: camping as a family is never easy, but I also believe it is completely worth the trouble. Camping is one of those family activities that get better each time you do it. After the first trip, your family begins to get a sense of what it takes to go camping and as you learn what equipment and what locations will make your trip more enjoyable; camping becomes an addictive pursuit. Tents, sleeping bags, air mattresses, stoves, backpacks, generator, chairs, mosquito nets, and bear lockers are all the things (plus more) that you will have to look at and possibly purchase to go camping; but you look at it as an investment that will reap dividends each time you camp.

I believe it is also making a statement to your family as well that you are willing to sacrifice some time, some convenience and some cash to spend time with them. Camping is not your typical vacation in that work must be done in a team-like manner in order to accomplish some sense of comfort. As the adults, you and your spouse will bear the brunt of the workload until kids can gain a sense of what is needed and also the knowledge of how to accomplish that task. These are times of great teaching and learning when done with a sense of family togetherness as the goal. Camping can be rewarding in that in addition to family time, families are out in nature enjoying God's created beauty, seeing animals they would probably never see elsewhere and families are having fun making crazy camp recipes like S'mores and hot dogs roasted on a stick. These are times where after the initial set-up on the first day is accomplished that makes camping all the more worthwhile.

And for those who feel tent camping is not their deal; then RV's are a great alternative. Whether purchased or rented, RV's can bring some of the comforts of home out into the wilderness for a near tent-like experience without all the hassle and worry of sleeping in a tent. Either way, in a tent or in an RV, camping is a great time to bring families together.

20

Meet your children's teachers and stay in close contact with them during the school year

Growing up, the last thing I wanted my parents to do was to meet and talk with my teachers. Why? Because, I was always getting in trouble. Why? Because my parents weren't staying in close contact with my teachers. See the pattern? Because of this issue, I never discussed with my parents what was happening at school because I was afraid of what would happen if they found out I was struggling or I was in trouble. This created a tension that built up until report cards came and then the roof blew off the house. This was something I did not want to pass on to my own kids.

When my kids started school, I made sure to meet their teachers. I made sure they knew who I was, how to contact me in as many ways as possible. I made sure they knew that education was important to our family and if there ever were struggles they were free to contact us at anytime.

The positive effect this has had on my immediate family vs. my home of origin family has been huge. Because our children know their teachers have an open path of communication to my wife and I, our kids know they walk a very thin line before we are notified of something going wrong with their academic life. This also has removed the tension I used to wrestle with; freeing my kids up to worry about more important things like what we are having for dinner. What I am saying is that if you are more involved in your child's academic life, they will actually do better in school and they will enjoy life and their family even more. The side bonus is the relationships we have had with our children's teachers have been amazing. My wife has begun friendships with a number of our children's teachers that move past our kids even attending school there any longer.

21

Play board games together

In this age of video games, board games have taken an unfortunate place in the back of the hallway closet or entertainment unit. It was destined to happen, all these parents today raised on a steady diet of Pong, Asteroids, Galaga, Nintendo, and then eventually Playstation; and this is only through the early nineties. Parents today with their kids have a great selection of electronic challenges to stimulate and entertain while satisfying the need to hang out together. But board games offer something different, something almost unique anymore; a time to challenge, laugh, strategize and communicate together without watching something that plugs into a wall socket or requires 16 D batteries for a half an hour's enjoyment. Sorry, Monopoly, Life, Clue, and Trouble; these are all great board games from the not-so-distant past that still can brings hours of enjoyment for families; and that is really what we are after: time together.

Board games can cause us to enjoy one another's company (if we aren't too hung up on always winning). Board games can allow us to deal with humility in a safe environment without the danger of feeling embarrassed. It also allows our families to deal with being a good winner. Board games give us time to spend with one another in a fun manner.

A friend of mine, a Mormon, has board game nights once a month with his family. Although he and I have differing views of theology, I appreciate his desire to have a family that is close. One of the students in my jr. high small group asked if we could have a board game night; yes, kids still enjoy these archaic relics. Put the Wii away and enjoy each other around a board game; see how fun a blast from the past can be. Maybe you'll even expand from board games and buy a set of Uno cards, a backgammon game or a checkers board.

22

Celebrate birthdays together

It's unfortunate that in my household growing up, birthdays were not that important. My wife's family was completely different; in their home, every birthday was viewed as a reason to celebrate. And not just with parents and mom and dads; but aunts, uncles, grandparents and cousins; it's a big deal. Dinner, presents, birthday cake, happy birthday song and lots of talking; it's really a big deal. When I turned 35, the students, parents and others in my church including my own family threw me a huge surprise party (I really was surprised) and it made me appreciate the fact that birthdays are important for the person celebrating and the person celebrating with them; that was a big deal!

And isn't that the way it should be, a really big deal. Another year of life and another year of blessings to be thankful for. I've become someone who now believes that no matter what is going on, no matter how busy we are, no matter what our economic situation, birthdays will be celebrated in our household. I want my kids to grow up appreciating each year of life and realizing that life is precious and we can't take it for granted and we need to be thankful for another year of life.

And my kids know it's special; letting our kids pick the restaurant they want to eat at; letting them bring a few friends to celebrate with us, saying a special prayer of thanks for them and their life, reminding them of how special they are in our lives, telling them once again what we saw and thought when they were born; these are all things we do when we celebrate birthdays together. I feel I will know this experiment with birthdays is a success when as a grandparent I am over at my kid's house and they are celebrating their children's birthdays the way we demonstrated for them.

23

Create legacy moments

Have you ever stopped and looked at your family and wondered what your children will be like when they grow up. What will they take with them? What will they do with their children that you do with them? How will they share with their kids why they do certain things because of how they grew up and what they saw? No matter what you do in life with your family, you will leave a legacy; it is either going to be good or it's going to bad. It will either be planned or it will be randomly put together. And so there is no confusion, I'm not talking about your estate or the business you have built up; I'm talking about the moments in time you created that will get passed on. It's unfortunate that some of us have already passed on some things that are going to cause our children and their family some heartache later; but I believe, we can overshadow most mistakes with an overwhelming of goodness, forgiveness and love.

Helping the less fortunate, caring for the elderly and the widows, taking my family on mission trips, going to church regularly (but not legalistically!), giving charitably, opening our home regularly for church and community events; these are our legacies that we will pass on to our children. Day to day life will occur regardless, legacy is something that is understood as important enough to plan and to see the bigger picture of the value this can create for our family. It also gives us things to do as a family that that are done mostly in the name of love, charity and family.

24

Celebrate accomplishments

After her first month at jr. high, my 7th grade daughter came home and shared with her mom and I that she had been chosen as Student of the Month. For our family this was made into a big deal; why? Because my daughter deserved to know that when she accomplished something great, she deserved to feel special. Dinner, some praise and shopping; she worked hard and we felt honored to heap a little reward on her.

As parents, we need to look for those moments, because most of the time, those moments are too few apart.

Kids will always look to see if we recognize their shining moments. Anytime my son makes a good play or gets a homerun, and anytime my daughter makes a great play on the soccer field, they always (ALWAYS!) looks to see if we were looking and we want them to know they are the center of attention when we are at their games and we are ready to celebrate with them when they play well.

Grades, sports, school awards, dance recitals, piano and musical concerts; these are all places where our kids are being recognized; it's important we let them know we are right there with them and we are excited and happy to be present. This sends an important message to them that we value their lives and we value the accomplishments that they are achieving.

25

Talk about your family tree and where your family descended from

Lets face it, we all came from somewhere; we all have a family tree and descendants who are our relatives from a long time ago (and not so long ago). It's easy for families to get an isolated view of family and only feel their immediate family is worth discussing and forget to include the rest of their family in discussions concerning family values and heritage. This unfortunately causes a family to have a myopic view of how big and how valuable a family actually is.

With the exception of my faith, I feel there is nothing more important in this world then my family; both my immediate and my extended family. If my kids grow up and they choose to isolate themselves away from family because it was not made clear enough how important this part of their life is, then I believe my wife and I will have failed.

Discussions about countries of origin, when our families came to America, the way they got here, who died young and who lived a long life, where parts of the family live now; these are all things we have discussed with our kids. Similar to attempting to expand our children's worldviews, expanding their family of origin views allows them to see life and family on a bigger scale. It also helps them to realize that someday, someone in the family will be talking about them in a similar manner. This, I believe will give them a greater sense of family and what role they will play in that family.

26

Subscribe to Rolling Stone and discuss bands that your kids are listening to

Fall Out Boy, Switchfoot, the Jonas Brothers, Flo Rida or Death Cab for Cutie; even if you don't these names, there's a good chance that your kids (ages 9-18) know these bands; and what's better yet is that they have them loaded onto their MP3 players and they are the ones that have your kids attention as they share their view on life to the world. Bands exist to entertain and to make money; that is their world. Pre-teens and teenagers are the biggest market for these artists and they make sure your kids have every chance possible to hear them. Commercials, video games, popular TV shows and movies, videos and concerts; music is big business and your kids are targets.

Unfortunately for kids, having them listen to the music isn't enough to satisfy the industry, they want kids to identify. Different genres of music exist, because different people relate in different ways; it was no different for us when we were teenagers. New-wave, punk, rock, rockabilly, and disco were all part of what we listened to when we were our kid's age; and we each listened for different reasons. Understand this: our kids listen to certain music because of certain reasons. If your child is solid in their understanding of who they are though, they probably listen for enjoyment purposes. If they are not solid in their understanding, they are listening to have the ability to relate to something that will help them create an identity. Which is why knowing who the bands are that are out there become so important. But, short of spending a ton of money on iTunes or at the local record store, what can a parent do?

First of all, you can take an interest in your kid's music. What is on their player, should be on yours as well. Nothing on my kid's iPods has not been listened to by me first. My kids know that if there is bad language or degrading suggestions toward the opposite sex, they won't get to listen to that music. The other thing that is good to do is subscribe to Rolling Stone. Rolling Stone does a great job of covering all different genres of music and will give you a healthy understanding of what the more popular bands are and what they are about. You might think your kids will rebel because this is an area that they want to hold sacred and to themselves; that would be an indicator that something else has broken down. In my experience, working with parents who have done this, it opens doors because it shows you are interested on more then a judgmental level; you are actually interested in something they are interested in on a cerebral level. Books have been written on this topic, but taking the first step and showing interest through study will go a long way in making music a bonding part of family rather than a divisive factor.

27

Create a family blog together to keep other families updated on your family's status

In this day of peer-to-peer interfacing, blogs are becoming as commonplace as a website or a Starbucks on the corner. MySpace and Facebook are the more popular personal blogging sites for the entry level users with blogspot being a little more for the advanced user. Anyway you choose it, people are using blogs for everything from marketing and advertising to espousing political rhetoric to keeping others updated on what bands they are listening to and what books they are reading. Another cool thing I see families doing is using the blogosphere to share with others what their family is doing and connecting with other family in different parts of the world or families that have similar family values.

Now before you think you could never put together a blogsite because of your non-techie background; understand that these sites are typically made for people like you and I to access and have the ability to put up our own blogsite. Blogsites are usually easy (and mostly free or low-cost) to setup and maintain. Adding text or pictures and graphics is usually fairly simple and most blogsites have help available to walk you through getting done what you want to get done. But how does this value your family?

Like any hobby, different people in the family can take different roles based on their strengths. For those who are good writers, they can provide the text updates. For those who have the ability to take and edit photos, they can use those to spice up the site. For those family members who have the ability to create graphics or have some layout knowledge, they can be in charge of that area. Everyone can help with this project and it gives family and friends the opportunity of staying connected to your family when connecting isn't always possible. This becomes an ongoing project that can give your family plenty of opportunity for discussion and moments working together.

28

Create Family walking stones and plant in your yard

In staying with her incredibly creative aunt last year, my daughter made a walking stone that was decorated with mosaic tile pieces in a beautiful design. Now, I say walking stone, but what it actually is, is concrete poured into a mold and then decorated before it dries; regardless, it looks really cool. That decorated stone soon found a place in our front planter and has become part of the landscape.

Our dog of 12 years just recently died and because he was such a huge part of our family we wanted to do something to commemorate his life in our lives. We decided to create walking stones to honor his life. We went down to the local craft store and found kits for the walking stones (approximately $15 each). In the kit came everything to create the stones: cement, mold, mixing stick and directions. My kids took their stones very seriously and created beautiful memorials for their dog Kanan, which had been such a blessing in their own lives. My son took the dog tag and embedded it into the stone and decorated it with drawings of him and the dog. My daughter wrote a poem and wrote that on the stone along with decorations she drew. These stones also became a part of our landscape and they became a tribute to our dog that we all miss very much.

In addition to the idea of a memorial for our dog, these stones gave us a chance to share in something together; a family project. We shared in moments of discussion and planning. We talked about Kanan and we talked about life and death. But we also thought and talked about the idea that these stones will be around for a long time and they are part of who we are as a family; they describe part of our family story. Whether it's a memorial or a special day you are celebrating or even a stone depicting each person's uniqueness; creating family walking stones create an art piece that will be treasured and admired by the whole family and anybody seeing them.

29

Grow a garden together

I want to be honest with you; I've never done this with my own family; but I want to. Growing up, my grandfather had the biggest garden I have ever seen. He had a huge parcel of land and half of his entire backyard was filled with garden. I remember as a boy being out there with him and helping him in various ways. Weeding, picking fruit or berries, trenching for new crops, watering and pruning were some of the things I got to do to help him. I loved that garden; it taught me about life in a different way then textbooks, TV and urban observation. It showed me the cycle of life, the pests, the difference a season makes and how hard work can pay off. That garden gave me a view of life that could only be achieved by getting my hands dirty and tasting something I helped grow.

When I look at my family, I am always on the prowl for a life lesson that I don't have to necessarily teach; something that is caught rather then taught. Gardens have the ability to teach some of those lessons. They help us remember to be thankful for the food we have because it doesn't get to our tables easily; somebody worked hard to get it there. It teaches us that things like bad weather can have a drastic effect on the food supply. It also teaches us there is a reason we pay so much money at the grocery store. Gardens are agriculture, economics, adult living and Earth science rolled into one big life lesson that we can pass on to our children. Whether you live in a house with some extra space to be able to do this or you live in an urban area that you share a space with others in a community garden; gardens can be a combined blessing of bonding moments and also help to the family food bill.

And I do think the biggest blessing for this idea is the time spent with family making the garden a success. Gardens can be a lot of work but each family member can have the opportunity to contribute to it's bounty, while at the same time enjoying one another's company and appreciating one another's hard work. The garden will also create memories that will have long lasting pictures of family togetherness. The biggest blessing for me in remembering my grandpa's garden was the time I spent with my grandpa and even though he has been gone for many years now, I can always remember that time as if it were yesterday; whenever I see someone with a garden, my thoughts go back to those fond memories my grandpa helped grow.

30

Read a book together and discuss

My wife and I are huge believers in the idea that leaders are readers. In both of our children we are proud of the fact that we have instilled in each of them a desire to read books and find enjoyment in what they are reading. This sometimes means that we have to purchase new reading material and that we need to see that as an investment rather then an unnecessary expense that causes us to feel burdened. We both also believe that whatever academic success they have (both of our children have blessed us with many great report cards and comments by teachers) has come as a result of our emphasis on reading as much as possible.

But in addition to providing reading material for our children, we believe we also need to model for our children what it feels like to discuss a story with others who have read the same story. Just like discussing a movie, discussing a book with others gives us the chance to see others points of view. This allows children to form an expanded worldview when they can see others perspective. It also helps our children to see the value of explaining what they read; this interpretive ability becomes important as they progress through school. Both of our children have shown an enormous propensity to read and understand at levels 3-4 years ahead of their peers.

But I think more importantly then academic success is the opportunity to spend time together as a family. Having a family book club gives us another chance to share time; which my wife and I believe should never be taken for granted and always be looked at as an important family value. When families share healthy time together, I believe there is always success. It may not be immediately apparent, but it will reap benefits as time goes on and more time is spent with each other.

31

Build a model together

When I was a kid growing up, I loved building models; funny cars, dragsters, hot rods, ships and planes; I built them all. But building models was usually a messy deal because no one really spent time with me showing me how to apply glue sparingly and how to wait to continue until the paint at least dried. My models would end up looking like a train wreck because parts would fall off because the glue wouldn't set on top of wet paint and people would ask me what the model was supposed to be. As I got older and I continued to build models on my own, I learned that patience was a necessary virtue of any good model builder and that most models took at least 2 weeks to do the right way.

When my son got to the age where models became a possibility for us to do together, we set off to build something of significance and something of lasting constructive integrity. Our first project together was PT-109, John F. Kennedy's boat that was sunk in World War II; which also made him a national hero. We spent hours painting all the detailed pieces, all the men on the crew and the hull itself. We made sure to let the paint dry and we then began the construction. I showed him how to sparingly apply the model glue with toothpicks so that he wouldn't get glue stringing out everywhere. After the construction was complete, I showed him how to cut, soak and apply the decals that went on the vessel (I can't believe they still do it that way). All in all, the model took us close to four weeks to complete; it still sits proudly on a shelf in my son's room. We next began construction on the Titanic; which is a whole other story.

These projects are great because it first gives us time to spend together; which should never be taken for granted. Next, it allows us to talk about the history behind the project and why it has significance. Finally, it gives me an opportunity to pass on the skill of model building which in itself is one of patience and direction following. For my son and I, this has been a time of great bonding (although building models has taken up a very small portion of our lives). What is also great about model building is that they come in different levels; from beginner to the very advanced; so anyone can do it. Local hobby shops, the internet and craft stores all have great selections of models and of model construction materials and supplies. This is a great hobby that can be shared with parents and children and it has lasting value in time shared, lessons learned and skills passed down.

32

Throw a holiday party for your children's friends and classmates

Because of a youth ministry background, throwing a party for a bunch of kids isn't all that difficult for me to handle. Send out invitations, buy a bunch of food (mostly sugar-laced), put together some crazy games, don't worry about the house getting thrashed, and meeting parents when they drop off their kids; that's pretty much all there is. But why do it? Why put yourself (and your family) through this for the sake of your kids? Because it gives them a chance to be a hero with their peers.

Why a hero? Kids lead pretty busy lives and our kids are no different. Soccer and baseball practices, homework, church activities and all the other stuff that fills the cracks of time; our kids get pretty busy. When something out of the ordinary happens (like a party with their friends) it gives kids a break from their everyday life and allows them to enjoy one another and enjoy someone else's hospitality. It's also amazing to see kids open up and let loose a little when given that opportunity; we in the adult world call that socialization.

When your child hosts a Halloween, Christmas, Fall, Winter, St. Patrick's Day, End of the school year party, they become a celebrity. They are viewed as the cool kid because they are doing something for the good of all their friends. It gives your child an opportunity to plan something and be responsible for something out of the ordinary. It also gives us as parents, an opportunity to share with our children what good hospitality vs. bad hospitality looks like. Why parents and responsible adults need to be present; why kids can't play spin the bottle; why music laced with profanity will not be allowed; why we have to keep the lights on; why we need to socialize with everyone we invite; these seem trite and possibly questionable, but they are a big deal to your child to understand in their development as maturing young people. I believe it also allows them to compare what their parents are doing for them vs. what others parents are doing for their children.

But returning to the hospitality idea; this becomes important as your kids get older and begin to determine how much are they willing to do for others. Are they willing to give to others, to sacrifice for others, to open up their home and share a meal with others; having these type of opportunities will enlarge their worldview of what they can possibly accomplish in the service to other people. Throwing a party for your children's friends may seem like an inconvenience, maybe a burden, maybe unnecessary; but to your kids it will help them in the shaping of their world in how they perceive the importance of others and their understanding of others perception of them.

33

Have a slurpee drinking contest

Okay, this is just plain silly; and that is the point. The first time I did this was a really hot day and I did this with 30 kids at youth group. I emptied the Slurpee machines at 7-11 only to turn around and there were 8 angry people behind me in line (in my defense, they weren't there when I got in line). There are places in the development of our kids, that they need to see adults in their life doing something that is random and fun. Riding a swing at the park, climbing trees (safely), letting our daughter make us over; these are just silly and fun ideas that have behind them a purpose of showing what spontaneity looks and feels like; that it's alright to have fun; even as responsible and mature adults.

All kids seem to love Slurpees; especially on hot days. The 7-11 in our neighborhood has about 7 flavors to satisfy anybody's taste desires. What is funny about this contest is that no one is immune to a brain freeze during a Slurpee race; everyone gets one. If you don't get one, chances are you aren't drinking fast enough. Watching kids roll around in misery and having them watch us in our misery is a funny site worthy of video footage.

Kids enjoy a challenge that they might actually win, so make sure you keep the sizes appropriate. Adults should be drinking larges vs. children's small or mediums. Good luck and remember: brain freezes can be tempered by pressing your tongue up against the roof of your mouth.

34

Create a scavenger hunt and then go with your children to figure it out

I need to warn you ahead of time that creating a scavenger hunt takes an investment of your time, but the payoff is huge. Scavenger hunt, treasure hunt, car rally; it's all very similar and kids love figuring out clues to fun, real life mysteries. Of the 20 or so of these I have concocted for youthwork purposes, I have never regretted any of them; they were all fun. With my own kids, the fun is double, because even though I know the answers, I love watching them have a-ha moments.

Setting up a scavenger hunt isn't really that difficult. First, you need to figure out the location; either a geographic area (like a city) or a specific location (like a mall or an amusement park). You need a starting point (your house or your child's school) and an ending point (usually a restaurant). Next you need to know how much time to scavenge for clues (10 clues equals 30-45 minutes). I typically make my clues to rhyme (it's a gift) and I have the clues running them around until they get to the final destination. Creating the clues takes approximately 4-6 hours of setup time. Have them find answers to questions looking for random stuff in the area you are playing. Sale signs, wording on menu boards, calories in a Juice It Up item, the number of stairs going up to a certain area; these are all just ideas that are endless when you start making up the clue sheets. The key is to keep it fun and possible for all kids playing.

If you want to break your family into teams, you denote the starting and stopping times; stagger the start times so everyone is not tripping over each other and ripping each other's answers off. You can add themes to the scavenger hunt (Pirates, Holidays, Seasons, celebrations, etc.) to add some spice to the scavenger hunt. You can give teams disposable (or loaded Polaroid) cameras to chronicle their adventure; the possibilities can stretch far, but the fun will always be remembered. Make sure to award the winning team with a fun prize for each contestant.

35

Get together with a few other families and do a progressive dinner

Okay, for some of you, you need Progressive Dinner defined. A progressive dinner is a multi-location dinner that each site (house) provides a different part of a meal. So the first house would provide hors D' oeuvres; the second house would provide salad, third house would provide main course and fourth house would provide dessert. This can be done with breakfast, brunch, or lunch as well as dinner. This also can be stretched out or minimized to fit whatever group size you have as well.

This can become a great family together moment with other families because no one person (or family) is solely responsible for the whole meal. It also gives a chance for multiple families to practice hospitality together. Kids have a chance to see other's homes and adults have a chance to share meals together with other adult friends and their kids.

It also allows our children the opportunity to see us having fun with others, doing something that is hardly ever done in the adult world. It gives us as parents the chance to talk with our kids about the joy and pleasure we can achieve in spending time with other families and sharing different styles of food together. This gives our children a sense of adventure and freedom to creatively look for ways to enjoy other people's company; that it doesn't always have to be the way they have always seen it done.

36

Go go-karting together

Back when I was a kid growing up, one of my favorite memories was go-karting with my family. At the time, this was probably more for my step-dad's enjoyment then our own, but we still tried to have some fun on his behalf. What I remember about go-karting was the idea of me being able to drive my own vehicle and show everyone in the world that at 8 year's old, I really did deserve to have my Driver's License. But in addition to the mad-skills that I possessed as a kart racer was the thrill of possibly beating my dad at his game (he once challenged another guy to a race backwards with us kids in the car for pink slips; he was a racer!) I never seemed to win him, but I always seemed to come really close; especially as my skills developed as a driver.

One of the things that seems to be forgotten about go-karts is the ability to teach basic driving skills in a fairly safe environment (I once was on a date and the girl plowed into the back of my kart and the body of her car completely disengaged and landed on top of me; we were both escorted off the track and told to leave; she had no skills, I married someone else). But really, go-karting is a time to challenge one another in the family, learn basic driving skills, and do something different and fun. With some of the new indoor tracks and the sleeker formula looking karts, training programs and official lap times; it has become more technical, and actually safer then ever. It also has risen to the level of a real-life video games; so in addition to the thrill of driving their own kart, kids get the thrill of being their own video game while getting them out of their video game chairs.

And getting the family out to do things is important; it helps your family to spend time together; no distractions to bother your time with each other; just you and your family; that's a precious jewel in your crown of life achievements. Whether it's go-karting, watching movies, or playing in the surf or snow; family time cannot be underrated or taken for granted. As I write this, my own children are ages 12 and 9; this time has passed by in the blink of an eye; I do not want to underestimate my time I have left with them; go have some fun with them, do something you've never tried before; you may find it's one of the best memories you ever create.

37

Bid on an ebay item that will benefit the family

My wife started it, I had nothing to do with it; in fact it scared me. But she would bid for these items on eBay and win them at great prices. It was kind of like bargaining for something in a foreign country; you throw out a price and somebody else throws out a price and maybe, just maybe, the seller accepts your offer or you flat out win because of time and you were the highest bidder; whatever the case, we, like many other people, were feeling the positive effects of shopping on eBay. One thing my wife has become in the last 18 years we've been married is a great shopper. Coupons, sales, and discounts; she'll find them and she will take full advantage. Ebay was one more extension of her seeking out great deals. This has crept over to our kids in now when they want something, they know we will try to find it on eBay first to see if we can get it cheaper then retail.

This has become a benefit to our kids in that they can now see the difference between retail pricing and possible discounted pricing elsewhere. Discounted pricing is now not some nebulous thought that we hope they will someday understand; it's sitting right in front of them in black and white and full-color. It also helps them to begin to understand budgeting in that we set a limit on how much we are willing to pay for something; sometimes we get the item, sometimes we don't, which teaches them how to deal with disappointment and control.

Disappointment in that we don't always get what we want and control in that we can't overspend past our budget in order to finally get that item. This allows us to teach and discuss with our children some great life lessons; disappointment is going to happen periodically throughout our entire lives and it's best to try to have a positive view on it; and control is necessary if we want to avoid the pitfalls of an over-indulgent lifestyle. Although it may seem you are trying to buy a new plasma TV, you are really teaching your kids some great life lessons in the process (so go buy that TV!).

38

Tell your kids you love them; daily

When school shootings were on the rise in this country, I remember one dad, who's daughter had tragically been killed that he had made a point throughout her entire life to tell her everyday he loved her. He still had to deal with the grief of losing his daughter, but he knew beyond a shadow of a doubt that she knew he loved her. I saw that and I remember thinking, that is important to do; I never want to regret not telling my kids I love them and mean it.

What does that mean, to mean it? I think it's important that if you choose to tell them, you don't do it to manipulate them or attempt to have them say it back just for you to feel satisfied that someone loves you. I don't want to bust chops, I want parents to understand that this is the most important thing you can say to your child; treat it with respect, value the opportunity to say it and appreciate the moment; it will be remembered.

It will be remembered when your child is struggling with his/her own problems; it will be remembered when your child is going through the stages of adolescent and adulthood development; it will be remembered when your child is on a date and someone else tells them they love them (they will now have something to compare that to). Our love for our children should never be implied, it should be overwhelming. This has nothing to do with spoiling your children, this has everything to do with letting your kids know they are the most precious people in the world to you and nothing else matters (in this physical world) like they do.

39

Let your children see you do affectionate things for your spouse

I kissed my wife yesterday in front of my two kids, my daughter laughed and my son got embarrassed. I do not hold back when it comes to holding hands, kissing in public, putting my arm around my wife, buying my wife little things like Godiva chocolates or lattes from Starbucks because I want my kids to see I am not ashamed of the woman I am married too and I will do little things (and big things sometimes) to show her. Frankly I am disturbed at how many couples who choose to show no affection around their kids because they feel it will send a bad message; a message of sensuality or even sexuality; trust me they appreciate it and need it more then we realize.

     Kids live in a world today where there is more divorce then commitment and longevity; they are put at ease when they see a healthy relationship between the two adults that are most important in their lives. They hear from their friends the pain they feel when their parents are struggling, your children live in the fear they could be next. When they see you leaving a card or doing something special for your spouse it sends a mental message to your children that all's well on the home front.

When we take it a step further and we do something based on one of our spouse's five love languages (author: Gary Chapman) we send a message that not only do we care, we care to do what will bring them the most fulfillment and satisfaction; this helps our children to see we do it for the other more so then just ourselves.

Affection is one the healthy outpourings of a good relationship. It needs to be monitored that it's not unhealthy for your kids to see (that's why we have a lock on our bedroom door), but good affection will teach your kids how they should treat and expect to be treated by others when they are in a serious relationship.

40

Put notes of encouragement and love in places where your kids can find them during the day

My wife is really good at this: random notes of encouragement and love in places where kids least expect it. Lunches, suitcases when they travel, under their pillows; my wife has surprised our kids on a number of occasions and they always are pleasantly taken aback. Spontaneous notes of love and encouragement are a great way to show your children you are thinking of them and that you want them to have a great day.

But in addition to reading a note of love and encour–agement, your children are being reminded of the special place they occupy in your life. That you would take time from a busy schedule and that you would do something small and special just for them.

It also elevates your children to special status with their friends. I believe all kids when they witness good parenting from another family are slightly envious that they couldn't have those parents for their own (unless they have great parents themselves). Your children become examples of what it looks like to live in a good family that cares enough to do the special things. Even if your child's friends don't experience this type of positive encouragement and love in their own home, they still can choose to do it with their own kids someday.

41

Talk about your dreams and ask your children for their input; listen to your children's dreams and comment positively on them in return

Our kid's world is partly lived in fantasy; they have that option and it serves them well. They have the ability to think abstractly because the world that has been built around them is not made of concrete walls; it's more like a sandcastle, that is a little unsafe, constantly shifting, but remarkably cool when you look at it from afar. Our kids are in a world where technology, where worldview and where relationships are constantly changing and redefining themselves. When we bring ourselves into their world and we begin to share what our dreams look like and what difference those dreams make, we begin to talk to our kids in a language they understand. We begin to show them that we have not resigned ourselves to living in any certain way and that we are always open to a better way of living our lives; for our sake and for the sake of others.

And helping our kids understand how the world operates and how dreams drive much of what happens in life helps them understand it's okay to think organically as opposed to linear. Thinking in a linear direction is fine when doing math homework or when one paints the outside of their house; but plans for the future need to be organic with room to evolve and grow. Helping our kids see what place dreams have in helping us to get where we finally are going is an underrated, but very important role parents play.

When kids talk to their friends, much of their time is spent talking about dreams they have. Sharing your dreams with them then gives them the opportunity to share their dreams with you. This can be a challenge if your kids share something that is not only out in left field; it would be bad if your child pursued it. Give your kids plenty of wiggle room when listening to them about dreams; most of what they share will not come to fruition, but with your encouragement and direction, some of it could come true. Dreams are a great starting place for what will possibly become a great starting point. Every great invention, every great building constructed, every great innovator, every great book written, every beautiful song sung or played started with a dream; never underestimate yours or your children's because that is where greatness begins.

42

Pick a family that needs help during the holidays and be the stealth family that helps them

This is a great idea that will not only help families in need who are struggling, but will send a huge message to your children about helping others. It's fun to watch my kids when we take on a project to help other families. They both become superheroes in thinking about possible ways to help and also sacrificing what they have or what they might get in order to help other people.

Finding families in need is easier then most people think. Think through people at work, at your child's school, sport's team, etc. If you don't know anyone or can't find anyone, call a local church or rescue mission; they are never short on needy families. Other ways to help are through organizations like Project Angel Tree or Operation Christmas Child; both are great programs that are doing an amazing job of helping out people in need at the holiday time.

The other part of this idea is to be stealth in helping these unfortunate others; why? Not just because I believe there is a special blessing for people who pass on the earthly reward of someone praising them for their helpfulness, but also, I believe it teaches our kids to do the right thing regardless of the reward they will receive. This develops within them an understanding to help someone just because it is the right thing to do; rather then the opposite, which is, help someone because I will get something out of it. This idea teaches our kids to have compassionate, empathetic and helpful hearts; which flies in the face of what the world today teaches.

43

Go to a concert together

There's a pretty good chance that if your child wanted to go to a concert, it would be somebody you have never heard of or somebody you have no desire seeing or hearing. That is pretty much the dilemma of going to a concert with our children. That idea aside, going to a concert with your child can be a great shared experience.

Going to a concert together with your children, allows you to enter into their world, to hear what is on their iPod and what their friends are talking about. It allows you to see your children enjoying something that is very close to their hearts. It also allows you to see other kids enjoying the same thing and getting a perspective of what that demographic is looking and sounding like.

If you do your homework, it can also be a great time to discuss the band's lyrical contents and the overall message they portray. This does not have to be done in a condemning type attitude, but in a dialogue type format; where your child is given the chance to come to their own conclusion.

On a reciprocal note, going to a concert with your children can give you the opportunity to get them to come with you and listen to a band that you like as well. This may not be such a big deal to you, but it will mean a lot to your children later on in life as they explain their eclectic view on music and artist appreciation. Having them with you as you enjoy your favorite genre of live music gives your children an exposure that they probably would never get on their own until they were much older. Going to a concert together with your children allows each of you to hear the world you each enjoy listening to.

44

Christmas carol in a convalescence home together

Christmas is a special holiday. I believe no other holiday has the significance, the effect, the family togetherness, and the magic that Christmas holds. But unfortunately for some, it is a sad and lonely time. For many senior citizens, whether living on their own or even in a convalescence home; Christmas is a stark reminder of how lonely their life has become; whether they have no one else or because their family has chosen to ignore them.

What a great opportunity for you and your family to spread some Christmas cheer by making the statement that you have not forgotten them; that they are loved and that they are important. Christmas caroling is a great way to share that Christmas spirit with those who need some cheering up. But how would you go about doing this?

First, you need to find a convalescence home in your area. Call the activities coordinator and tell her/him what you would like to do. Show up at the arranged time and check in. Most convalescence homes have no problem with a family going down the halls singing Christmas carols (unless it's June). Have preprinted song sheets and practice beforehand so your kids can get used to singing the songs. For added fun, ask other families to join you. Complete the night by going back home and enjoying some hot cocoa together and talking about the different people who touched their hearts in different ways.

45

Go to the beach together

Living in Southern California, the beach is part of our life. We love playing in the surf, laying in the sand, the smell of the salt in the air, and enjoying the restaurants on the water. In fact, my wife and I were engaged on Balboa Island after a dinner at Ruby's on the Newport Beach pier. It's just part of who we are.

When we go to the beach, we know there's a lot to do while we are also relaxing. Sand castles that must be built, seashells that must be collected, bodies that must be buried, and waves that must be body boarded; this is a fun and sometimes busy day, but it is always fun.

If going to the beach some things that are necessary to bring are sunblock (SPF 30 at least), sand chairs, blanket to lay on, towels, sand toys, body boards, changes of clothes, hat or visor, and a small cooler with drinks and snacks. Remember: If your kids are not aware of how powerful the surf can be, always stay close by and watch them; the waves can be unpredictable and can not only knock children (and adults) down, it can drag them back out to sea. With small children, it is always better to set up by a lifeguard tower in case of an emergency.

46

Work on a school project together

Depending on your child's school, this may not be an option for you. My children attend school, where parent participation is expected, so we don't get a choice. But after assisting to build numerous science projects, missions, models and display boards; I've learned that there is a lot of fun to be had by helping your child with their school project. It is also an opportunity to share some time with your child on a project that will help them with their grade in a particular class.

Lest you become one of those parents that build the entire project on your own and sign your child's name; you need to remember some important rules when helping your child. First, it is your child's project; you are merely helping them complete it. Second, your role is to provide material acquisition, preparation guidance, positive constructive criticism and transportation assistance. You should always let your child complete as much of the project on their own with you only assisting where necessary. Sometimes this may include cutting with a saw or x-acto knife, painting with a brush or spray can, gluing with various types of adhesives and arranging the project to look as authentic and masterfully completed as possible. This requires much self-control on the parent's part, because your child may not have the best looking project in the class; but he/she will have a good-great project that they were largely responsible for; which is typically what the instructor wants. And isn't that the goal? If it's not the goal for you, then this is where we have the little talk about your child's development and how much they need you to allow them to grow on their own and the thought that if we constantly are doing their work for them, eventually they will fail and we as parents won't have anyone to support us in our old age; so don't do the project for them.

47

Build and fly kites together

Okay, I'll be honest; this one is on my to-do list also. My daughter and I flew kites together once and it was kind of a disaster; but that has not deterred me. We have a great field across the street from our house and I always see people out there on windy days flying their kites with their kids.

But for me, the excitement is more in the preparation for the day you will go out and actually fly your creation; which means more commitment then the store bought variety. If one desires to build and fly kites, one must learn from those who have already done this. In another words, you will need to look on the internet or buy a book that shows you how to build a kite; a simple Google search of "building a kite" yielded 328,000 results; finding out how to build a kite does not seem all that difficult. Next you will need to buy the materials; most hobby shops and craft supply stores should have the necessary materials to construct a kite worthy of flight. All that is left now is the construction and the flight.

As with all the steps, make sure to include your kids in order that they might enjoy the minute details with you; they will appreciate the final objective (flight) more when they participated in all the steps leading up to it.

48

Swap ipods for a weekend and comment on each other's music (positive only)

In this day of technology, one of the greatest inventions that have changed the face of an industry has been the iPod. Although there are other MP3 players, they collectively don't come close to the market share that iPods possess; it seems everyone has one. It's interesting to get on a plane and see how many people listen to iPods while traveling.

Most parents I know today have iPods just like their kids. Parents may not spend as much money on their music as kids do, but both parents and their kids spend plenty of time with their headphones on listening to the music that brings them pleasure. Just like our lives when we were kids, music is very important to kids. Entering into this area of their life should be done carefully with careful regard to why they choose to listen to certain music styles and artists.

Trading iPods with your kids for a weekend gives parents and adults an opportunity to dialogue why they enjoy certain artists and styles of music. It allows you to share with your children what certain music styles and artists remind you of and gives you the chance to ask them the same. It also gives you the chance of possibly hearing a band that you may like (and vice-versa) which then gives the two of you some common ground.

49

Go to the county fair and share a deep fried Twinkie

I'm not really a guy who enjoys deep fried food. I would rather have something a little healthier by having it baked, broiled or raw; deep-fried is not the best deal if you are trying to live healthy. Now there are exceptions; fried chicken once in a while would be one of them. Another exception is the country fair and all the fried delicacies they have to offer. Fried Twinkies, fried Snicker bars; I even saw deep fried Pop Tarts this last year. The good thing about these country fair delicacies is that not too many other restaurants in the world are serving these cardiac inducing treats; which makes going to the fair all the more fun.

Kids love deep fried foods and they like food that is sweet; what a great marriage the deep fried Twinkie makes. Sharing one of these treats with your kids is the equivalent of riding a rollercoaster or listening to one of their bands on their iPod; it's entering into their world and showing them you can still have fun.

People eat these deep fried heart attacks for no other reason then to say they've done it and to satisfy curiosity and a sweet tooth; and it's perfectly okay to indulge once in awhile. Kids have us as parents to offer boundaries and to keep them safe and healthy; but showing them it's okay to try something fun is a good step toward creating an adventurous child. It's also an easy way to introduce them to the idea that we need to not be afraid of trying different food in the world; whether it is sweet, ethnic, or different looking.

50

Go on a picnic together

Picnics don't seem to have the type of appeal that they may have once garnered in our culture; and yet there is something very wholesome and inviting about a picnic for the sake of family togetherness. Picnics are a great way to plan a day out and enjoy each other's company while not worrying about what is on the menu, getting a table or finding a space in the parking structure.

Picnics are a great time of getting out, eating some food, and enjoying each other's company. Picnics can be done at a local city park, at a larger state park, at the beach, in the mountains or in your yard; they can be very versatile. Picnics can be done on a blanket, on a table or on the tailgate of a truck or SUV. You can bring the food already premade or you can setup a BBQ and grill your meat onsite; small gas grills work better for this as you won't have to contend with hot coals afterwards.

Don't forget that while on a picnic, food is not the only thing to enjoy. Plan to enjoy your family's company with some fun activities as well. Flying kites, playing Bocce ball, throwing a Frisbee, playing catch, going on a hike or walk, swimming (if near water), board games and card games; these are just some of the possibilities. The main idea here is to get away from the hustle and bustle and spend time with one another enjoying each other's company.

51

Adopt a Compassion International child

Living in a country where most people's needs are fairly well provided for; it's hard to imagine sometimes that there are children in the world who go day to day without the basic necessities of life. Shelter, food, clothing and clean drinking water are a challenge for them and have been a challenge since the day they were born. Millions of people struggle in this world and if it weren't for organizations like Compassion International, they would never even have a fighting chance. Compassion provides educational opportunities, social development, basic life needs and spiritual direction for thousands of children everyday; but they don't do it alone.

Hundreds of thousands of people have stepped up and assisted Compassion with providing resources to these children who are the suffering innocents of the world. Through their Adopt A Child program, many people, including families have committed to providing monthly donations to help Compassion in helping these children. Many families have chosen to adopt a child through support and bring the child into their family by writing letters back and forth and by sending special gifts during the holidays. Although not mandatory, Compassion encourages supporting people to communicate with their adopted child and for the supported child to communicate back. Some families I know, have even traveled to visit their child and have helped them to continue in their education as they have gotten older.

This program is a great way to teach children what it means to reach past our comfort zones to help those in need (even globally). Although it becomes a family project, it becomes something greater in that a family is taught how to care for another human being. And although Compassion International is a Christian organization, a family does not need to be Christian in order to support this organization or to support it's mission of helping hurting children. You can learn more about their program at www.compassion.com.

52

Take a family cruise together

Cruising is not just for senior citizens any longer; taking a cruise as a family is a great way to spend time together and do something a little different in an attempt to draw your family closer. Cruising has some advantages over a typical vacation in that most activities are pre-planned in that you and your kids just have to show up. Food is also part of the package, where passengers just need to show up at their designated times and enjoy the ship's cuisine; although there is usually all you can eat food available at any time in certain areas of the ship. The disadvantage of cruising is that rooms are typically smaller then hotel rooms, possible motion sickness and the confinement of a ship; these items aside, cruising can be a great vacation.

Companies like Disney offer cruises to satisfy entire families. Special shows, opportunities and programs are geared for different ages of children as well as opportunities for adults. Family excursions and events are also a big part of their cruises.

If budgeting is an issue, families can plan their cruise during slow parts of the season or plan a smaller trip of a few days compared to an entire week or 10 days. Working with a travel agent will give you an advantage in that they will be able to alert you to anything you might need or any additional costs that could be incurred as you enjoy your vacation; they will also help you plan a cruise that will keep you within your budget.

53

Create a fundraiser together and raise money for a noble cause

This probably isn't your typical family idea to do together, but who said you have to be a typical family? The reality is there are a lot of great causes to raise money for in this world, you and your family just need to figure out which one is closest to your family's heart. But how does a family go about creating a fund–raiser after they deem a cause worthy enough to raise support for?

Support letters to family and friends, a Facebook or MySpace page devoted to your cause, selling something on eBay and giving the money to the cause, doing a small benefit dinner at your house in order to solicit donations; these are just but a few ideas that will help you raise funds for your cause. I had a student in my youth ministry once who raised $1200 in a week through a web advertisement in our pursuit of helping to assist with world hunger and poverty. The sky is the limit when creating a way to help others in need or assisting a cause that ultimately will help others.

For families, this creates an opportunity to grow together while helping others. It shows our children that we can put together something big that could seem out of reach, but with the right planning can come together and be an exciting way of lending a helping hand to humanity that needs some assistance.

54

Set a fun goal and start working toward it

People in life need goals, if they didn't have goals, they would never have any accomplishments to look back upon and enjoy the satisfaction of finishing something they planned and started. Families also need goals for the same reasons. Collectively, families need to be able to plan something and work together toward completion to be able to someday look back and enjoy it's conclusion.

In life there are working type goals (education, painting the house, job promotions, etc.) and there are fun goals (go on vacation, save for a special purchase for the family, visit all the American League ballparks before children turn 18, etc.).

As family, fun goals are a way to instill in our children in a fun way, what goal setting can do to help them through different points in life. It's also a way to unite the family for a common cause.

Fun goals also give our family a reason to think creatively and allow us to pull our resources toward the idea of completion. It's amazing to me in our family, when we set a goal toward something we all enjoy, how creative and how hard working my children become in order to complete that goal. It's important though, that when a family decides on completing a fun goal, that everyone has buy-in. Once everyone is on board, then we can all spur one another on toward doing our part to get the goal accomplished.

55

Go see a play together

The truth: I'm not much of a play watcher; but I should be. I should also be a dad that encourages his kids to be play watchers. Why? Because we as parents should do as much as possible to expose our children to the fine arts in order that they might grow in their understanding of the world and the arts that are within that world.

Plays give our children a chance to see a different form of entertainment that requires some imagination as well as appreciation for the gifts that the performers present.

Seeing a play together differs from seeing a movie in that the actors are present and that the set is fabricated in such a way that there are constraints on how close to realism they could come.

We've taken our children to a number of plays and to our surprise, they actually enjoy them. I think we as parents sometimes pass our biases on to our children and fail to give them the opportunity to see life from different angles; it's important as parents that we push past those biases so as not pass them on to our children. Plays are a great form of entertainment and children enjoy being entertained from various forms of media. Plays don't have to be expensive, many colleges and community playhouses put on family friendly plays at affordable costs; sometime cheaper then taking the family to the movies. The additional benefit to a play vs. a movie is that it teaches our children to sit quietly (most of the time) so as not to distract others and the actors who are enjoying and performing. It also creates great moments of discussion afterwards when sharing what were the parts that were really enjoyable to each person in the family that was watching the play.

56

Go to the mall together as a family

Okay, so this isn't really such a big deal; in fact, sometimes it's more hassle then productive; but if you have to go, might as well see the value in it. My family makes it to the mall a couple times a month and for us it's a way to people watch, keep up on consumer culture, stock up on necessities and grab a meal together. We don't really view the mall as necessary, but it makes killing time together a little easier.

Most of the time when going to the mall, it's with the idea that we'll be getting something to eat and look around some stores at the same time. When with our kids, we don't always go home with something in our hand; in fact most of the time, we go home empty-handed. This is important to understand that we don't feel like we always have to buy something to make a trip to the mall worthwhile. For us, it really is about finding another way to hang out together. For our kids, they have come to understand this idea and don't seem to mind as long as they can look at some of the things they may want to buy later cheaper online or on eBay.

The mall isn't always the best place to find great deals, but it is filled with lots of people that look very similar to us or very different from us; which is always good exposure for our children. It's the modern day marketplace that gives us a glimpse into the soul of our society. Seeing the culture we live in surrounding us is a great place to discuss with our children what it means to live in a diverse community where the landscape appears more as a mosaic as opposed to a paver. My kids have come to see life and community within this framework partly do to our visits to the local malls.

57

Make home made pizza together

Like most Americans, pizza is one our family's favorite foods. Whether ordering for delivery or eating out at our favorite pizza joint, we really enjoy eating a slice of pepperoni or even better: ham and pineapple. A couple of years ago, when our friend Brian made us homemade pizza, we began trying our hand at putting together our own pizza; and this has become one of our family favorites for dinner.

Homemade pizza is not as tough as it sounds and families can have fun making this recipe together; or each family member can make their own. My family uses the Bridgeford bread dough for the crust. My wife will thaw the dough to room temperature and allow it to rise. She will then spread it over a pizza pan and apply the toppings. For sauce we just use bottled spaghetti sauce; then shredded cheese, and meat and other toppings. Throw in the oven and within 15 minutes, you have your pizza(s). You can also cook it on the BBQ and get that flame-cooked flavor; either way, it tastes great!

The key here is preparing a meal you can all help with and one you will all enjoy. This is a great place to try varieties also (like BBQ sauce instead of spaghetti sauce and pre-cooked chicken). This is also a great place to invite other families over to make pizza; just have the bread dough ready to go and have the other family bring their own toppings.

58

Have a jump-roping contest

My friend Josh is an amazing jump roper. He actually has been all over the globe and in videos jumping rope; he's amazing. Jumping rope is one of those areas that our kids think they have the monopoly on (some of them actually do!). What's fun about jumping rope is that it is one of those skills like riding a bike that once you know how, you really don't forget how to do it

Challenging your kids to jumping rope is a small challenge that builds not only repoire with your kids, but allows them to see you doing something that they only usually see their classmates doing on the playground. It proves to your kids that you were young once also and that you have a playful side that comes out every once in awhile.

Not to take the challenge too seriously, you can challenge your kids to jumping rope the longest; who can do the most double and triple jumps; who can cross the rope the most and even some double-dutch action; if you're up to it. You can even see who can jump rope the longest on one foot instead of two or reciting something that you all memorize. A jump-roping contest is a fun way to enjoy each other and do something that kids aren't always use to seeing adults do.

59

Make ice cream together

Whether it's a hot day outside, on a plate next to birthday cake or on top of apple pie; ice cream is the best; and homemade ice cream is even better. Homemade ice cream is smooth and soft and typically the flavors are more noticeable because they've had less chance to evaporate or soak into the other products of the ice cream.

Like pizza, kids love making ice cream; to them it's like a science experiment to see if the cream, eggs, sugar, ice, rock salt and flavorings can make actual ice cream that tastes good. Recipes usually come with the ice cream maker and many recipes can be found on the Internet

Although the process can be done without an ice cream maker, an ice cream maker actually whips air into the mixture to make the ice cream lighter and fluffier. Since an ice cream maker is not used that often and can run about $100, ask a relative or good neighbor to borrow one before buying one. IF it's something your family enjoys doing, buy one in the off-season or on eBay where the price will be cheaper.

60

Decorate for the holidays

My family loves the holiday season. We love the festivities, the smells, the food, going to church services and the parties; but more then all these things, what really gets us in the mood for the holiday is the time we spend decorating our house together.

The tree, the lights, tree decorations, the table decorations, the candles, the wall hangings, the knick-knack items; these are all packed away in boxes and have to be carefully unpacked. This is something my wife and I could probably do faster without our children's help, but we choose to make this a family time together. A fire going in the fireplace, holiday music playing on the stereo; some hot cocoa or wassel; these are some of the things we do to set the mood for what will be the remainder of the holiday season. Unpacking and setting up the holiday decorations has become for our family a time of kicking off the joyous season and announcing to each other that we are excited for the holidays to be here and to be able to celebrate and spend time together.

Some families choose to minimize holiday décor for the sake of not having to put up in the beginning and cleanup in the end; kids notice this. The holidays are a special time and decorating is just part of the chore we take on to help our kids (and ourselves) feel the distinction that is in the air. Decorating is not to take away from the faith-based reason we celebrate, but it gives the holiday season some extra flair that makes it that much more special. The more a family chooses to decorate at the holiday time with their kids, the more their children will begin to look forward to the holiday season arriving; for all it's pleasantries, not just the presents they will be receiving.

61

Hand out full size candy bars at Halloween

This actually isn't my idea; I borrowed it from my friend Rick Bundscuh; I just liked it so much, it needed to be included on this list of 100. Halloween for us has typically been working at the church for one of our harvest outreach events (why can't we just call it Halloween?); but we have occasionally made it home early where we were able to hand out some candy. My kids love being the one to open the door and hand the candy; I don't know if it's their desire to act as the representative of the house, to get the first chance to see someone else's costume or to act graciously and hand out something they know the kids at the door want. Whatever it is; they are the hero when we give out candy.

And when a kid gets a full-size candy bar, there's something special about that house; that house is pegged as being cool; no rotten eggs being thrown at that house. What a great message also, to share with the neighborhood that this house represents generosity and appreciation for the neighbors. Full-size candy bars make a statement that you see the value in going big for the sake of others.

To our kids it also makes a statement; that we have a responsibility to go the extra distance in representing a loving and gracious home to those in our community. That even though others are content with giving bite-size treats, we want to have a bigger heart toward doing things for our community because that is at the core of who we are. The lesson here is when our kids see us doing something nobody else is doing in order to send a positive message; they feel empowered by their family to go and do things that are nice to send a message of love to their community.

62

Teach your kids how to paint a room the right way

Give a kid a paintbrush or roller and a bucket of paint and you will absolutely have a mess; it's inevitable, because paint is messy and kids don't know what to do to avoid that mess. Teaching a kid to paint a room is a life learned lesson of it's better to sweat in preparation then die in battle.

Painting a room in a house the right way is tough work; but it's a learned discipline that will last a lifetime. Taping a room off, covering the floor to avoid spillage, prepping the walls so the paint will stick the first time, using the proper roller with the right nap for your type of walls, having the can shaken at the paint store or stirring with a paint stick, cutting in the corners of the room with a brush first; these are some of the things that need to be taught and caught while showing kids how to paint a room the right way.

This is one of those life lessons that they can look back on and see where their hard work mattered; where they can see something done right versus the possibility of something done wrong.

Growing up, my mom was constantly painting different rooms in our many houses and apartments. I have not had to do this with my own children yet, but I have done it with plenty of the kids in my youth ministries. It's amazing to me how many kids think painting a room is license to have a paint fight; but that only happens once when they have to clean up their mess and they try to get paint out of their hair. When I've shown kids the right way, they are often amazed at the time is takes to get ready to paint and how little time it actually takes to paint the room. Passing this ability on to your kids will allow them to have a trade that they can use in their adult life as they work on their own homes (getting a room ready for you to come and move in with them).

63

Teach your child how to drive

You really shouldn't attempt this unless your child is at least 15-16 years old. With that being said, you also should think about teaching them in an automatic first before you move to the more challenging manual transmission (stick-shift). You should also refrain from driving on the street or highway until they have a learner's permit and instead find an empty parking lot somewhere where nobody will get hurt (just not my church where I could be walking).

That being said, teaching your child to drive is a great time to show your child you trust them enough to allow them to take your life into their hands. It is a right of passage that handled incorrectly can have serious implications on your relationship later; handled correctly, you become a hero for life. It's important that as the adult, you consider all the possible mistakes your child can make and prepare yourself mentally for how you will handle it when they make that certain mistake; sometimes over and over again. As you go through the list of preparations necessary to get ready to drive; share the possible common mistakes with your child to let them know you are aware that those things can happen.

This is also a good time to share with your child what it was like when you learned to drive; the mistakes you made and the nervousness and anxiety you felt. This will show your child that what they are feeling is also normal. Remember as you coach your child to driving greatness: how you react to the positive and negatives of their driving abilities will determine how nervous they are when they are on the road (someday with your grandchildren).

64

Ride the city bus or subway somewhere special

For some people, this is their regular mode of transportation, so it won't be that special. For us others who don't venture very far from our cars, riding the bus or subway are more of an adventure. With our kids, who always love adventure, this is a treat.

Most cities and suburban areas have a mass transit system; finding how where and how they run is usually just a matter of looking on the Internet at their website. Typically if a city has an interesting tourist destination or community hotspot; mass transit will find a way to get you there.

If you do need to do some research; having your kids help is a great way to begin to peak their interest. Talk to them about times when you needed to ride the bus or subway and what were some of the things you remembered (costs, location of bus stop, how far you walked after your bus ride, etc.).

When you go on your bus or subway ride, make sure to bring plenty of dollar bills and some change. Talk to your kids about proper etiquette when riding on public transportation and help them understand that there is nothing shameful about using public transportation (in fact, some people choose to use public transportation as opposed to driving their own cars)

Take the chance to share with your children how utilizing public transportation when possible is good for the environment and most of the time cheaper then utilizing your own car. You can also talk to them about Rosa Parks and dialogue with them about what that would feel like to live in a segregated time where even public transportation was segregated.

65

Take a tour of a presidential library

Presidential libraries are not libraries per se, but are actually repositories where presidential documents, articles, gifts of state and other items of importance to that certain president's term are stored and displayed. Presently there are 12 Presidential libraries in the U.S. with Massachusetts leading with 3 different libraries.

Presidential libraries are a great place to go with children to allow them to see and hear how important the Office of President is within our government. It also allows us a chance to talk with our children about the fact that despite the fact we may not agree with everything a certain president does; the position of President is to be respected by all Americans.

This gives our children a perspective of who we are as parents, but also who we are as Americans, despite our political affiliation. This helps them to see that in America, we have a system that has checks and balances. It also helps them to understand that the President is human, with shortcomings but also with the potential to do great and amazing things.

Viewing a presidential library with your children allows our children to see us within a bigger picture; whether we are Democrat, Republican, Libertarian or undecided; we are Americans first. Allowing ourselves to experience this history lesson with them allows us to have an opportunity to dialogue with them about the blessings we have in living in such a great country.

66

Go to a waterpark for a day

My first waterpark adventure was with my then 6-year old daughter, Emilee. She and I spent the day at Knott's Berry Farm's Soak City in Buena Park, California. This was a great day not just because we spent time together; but my daughter and I were able to experience some rides that gave us both a thrill as we rode them together; this was despite the fact that I thought I was putting my daughter's life at risk every time we got in another line.

As with any amusement type park, lines are just a way of life. But these lines were fun because we were standing there dripping wet and laughing at all the people screaming as they went down the chute, or swishing around the winding drop or tubing down the class-5 rapids. These lines were filled with lots of good interaction and moments of anticipation. I also found myself reassuring my daughter over and over again that she was going to be safe and that Daddy wouldn't let anything happen to her. This was good because in a way I became the hero every time she made it through a ride.

By the end of the day, after soaking up a day's worth of sun, riding on the water rides, tubing on the lazy river, we were both pretty well spent. But nothing could stop my daughter from sharing in excitement to her mom how much fun she had endured and how much she looked forward to going again. Since then, we have gone a number of times with both our kids and the scenes from the first trip seem to repeat themselves over and over again; it's my plan to milk this as long as my kids want to go and for as long as they aren't too embarrassed with me having my shirt off.

67

Bury a time capsule

I've watched schools do this, I've heard of businesses doing this, but I've never seen or heard of a family doing this; you could be the first! Time capsules are cool I think, if left long enough to incubate; long enough that what is inside is retro cool and fun when dug up. Mementos, a town newspaper, small favorite toys, a picture of the family pet, a menu from a certain favorite restaurant, a note from each member of the family on what is important to them at this very point in life (not to be read until opening day); these kind of things can be fun to revisit in 15 or 20 years.

And the reality is, time capsules mean nothing unless given that time to become special. Families need to designate a timed opening in the future; deviating only from the set time if a family moves or the spot needs to be dug up for a future building projects (like a cool family pool!); even then a family can choose to keep the objects inside the container until the day which has been designated.

Would there really be a point to this though? I think anytime families can generate some excitement about doing something together, then that item has some merit to be considered. Burying a time capsule takes a little bit of planning, but becomes a project everyone can get involved with. Care must be taken to find a suitable container that can withstand the elements underground; Rubbermaid containers with snap-on lids work well. Your family should make sure to set a date in the future when the container will be opened; maybe around a certain birthday or anniversary.

68

Make S'mores

I believe that as long as there has been chocolate bars, marshmallows, and graham crackers, there have been S'mores. One of my favorite lines in a movie is from *The Sandlot,* explaining to the main character: Smalls what s'mores are:

> "You're killing me, Smalls! These are s'mores stuff. Okay, pay attention. First you take the graham. You stick the chocolate on the graham. Then, you roast the mallow. When the mallow's flaming, you stick it on the chocolate. Then you cover it with the other end. Then, you stuff."

That's a great movie to watch with your kids and S'mores are a great treat to share with your family and a lot of fun preparing. Just like Cotton Candy, S'mores are one of those treats all kids seem to love, while most adults seem to tolerate them at best. S'mores are typically cooked over a campfire, but a BBQ, or a backyard firepit will work as well (I wouldn't recommend a fireplace inside the house; too dangerous and too messy). Keep in mind that hands and faces are going to get very sticky, make wet-type wipes available afterwards.

I think the take-away for S'mores is silly fun, but also some creativity as well. S'mores take work; not hard work, but still some work. Kids enjoy getting the ingredients together and with your input, they will have a great time making a culinary masterpiece.

69

Go sledding / tubing

A couple of years ago, my family and I went up to the mountains for a weekend. Our plan was to snowboard for two days and then come home. On the first day we took the kids up snowboarding and had a good time. We paid for the snowboard rentals, the lessons, the extra gear we forgot to bring and food; it was a good day; but a lot of work plus a lot of money.

On the second day, we decided to try and find something else to do; both of my kids had fun snowboarding but were really tired from the previous day. We found a tubing hill on the outside of town that completely changed our view of the extreme sport of tubing.

This tubing hill was first class; no stairs, this hill had an escalator all the way up. We bought each of us a lift ticket, grabbed a tube from the pile at the bottom and proceeded up the hill. This ended up being one of our funnest family events together; ever!

Tubing down the hill whether we connected all four of us together, or each went down on our own or racing each other, was a blast. Had you told me the day before we would have this much fun, I would have laughed out loud and I would have been wrong.

Tubing or sledding together can be a great family day because kids see parents taking some risk to have fun with their kids. Parents are put on equal footing as their children and anything can happen; including wipeouts; which kids love to see.

I feel the beauty in tubing or sledding is that there is really no skill involved. Everyone can have a great time as long as they are willing to climb up the hill (not in our case, though; we had an escalator). This side trip ended up being the best part of our family vacation that winter, and we still talk about the fun we had together.

70

Go ice blocking

If you don't know about this crazy, extreme-sport phenomena, ice blocking is similar to sledding in wintertime, except everything is opposite. Instead of sitting on an object in the freezing cold of winter and flying down a snow covered hill; you instead are sitting on an ice block with a towel draped over it in the middle of summer flying down a grassy slope. For adults you can fuse two blocks together by pouring salt on one side and butting it up to the side of another block; you then tie the two blocks together with a piece of rope (the rope also gives you something to hold onto). Cardboard also works well as a cover instead of a towel. Sounds crazy, doesn't it? And yet you and your children will have a blast trying this. Remember though, whatever goes down the hill must come back up the hill to ride it again; so don't make it too big.For extra fun, you can see if you can get your entire family down on a block.

Typically you go down feet forward sitting on your bottom so you can use your feet as brakes; if you are really daring go down head first lying on your belly. The thrills and spills are great times as you watch each other crash and burn on the grassy hillsides. Make sure to have a video camera to catch the action. If you want to see people trying this, check out ice blocking on www.youtube.com (make sure to screen all videos though before showing your kids).

71

Buy Airsoft guns and have "pinging" contests

First of all, what is an airsoft gun you may ask? An airsoft gun is similar to a BB gun except it shoots small plastic bb's instead of brass bb's. You can find them for sale in paintball shops and most sporting good stores. Although they can be dangerous if shot at someone (unless protective gear is worn) they are extremely fun and safer then actual bb guns. They can break the skin but only when shot at very close distances with the air pressure dialed way up Airsoft guns are modeled after most of the popular real models, but are distinguished from real guns (as all toy guns are) by a florescent-colored tip at the end of the barrel; never color or let your children color the tip black to make it appear real (this is to let law-enforcement know it is a toy).

"Pinging" is the sound an airsoft gun makes when hitting an empty soda can; so it is much like target practice; but seemingly safer. An airsoft gun shoots at enough velocity to knock over an empty can so contests can be had between members of the family to determine who is the best shot. Targets are also available at airsoft supplying stores that cause the plastic BB to actually stick to the target with a soft gel mat that then causes the BB to then drop in a box for use again later on (yes, you can reuse the bbs if they are not damaged or dirty).

Although I have no other guns in our house, I feel airsoft guns are a safe and fun item for the family to enjoy while spending time together. We always wear safety glasses or sunglasses while shooting to protect our eyes and we have never had an accident that causes us to question whether we should be doing this with our children (although I am sure it has happened somewhere).

72

Learn a slideshow program and create slideshows for your children's teams

Before the computer and digital cameras came to be, people would take pictures of things or places that were important to them and if they then wanted to share them with others, they would have their film developed as slides and display them through a slideshow, utilizing a slide projector. If one wanted to really be slick with their slideshow, they would utilize two projectors with a separate device that meshed the two slides together during the slide change transition and use music on a stereo for background enhancement. With computers and digital cameras now being so readily available, it has changed the way people share their pictures with others. Computers are amazing and they have allowed average people with no real training or education to put together and save brilliant digital slideshows. The potential is limitless on what you could do once learning these simple softwares.

With both of my children playing sports, I wanted to be able to do something for the team that not many other people had thought of; something to capture the magic of the season together. Taking my digital camera and snapping shots throughout the season of different kids on the team; I would work on a digital slideshow that I could give to every member of the team at the end of the season. Taking my shots and plugging them into a slideshow software (like PowerPoint or iPhoto) I was able to put together a slick slideshow complete with cool and seamless transitions, music and titles. I then burned the slideshow onto a DVD (through the program iDVD) and presented to each team member their own slideshow to play through their own DVD player. This was usually played at the end of the season party with all the kids and parents watching.

For my kids, this was fun in that they had editorial input as we worked on the slideshow. It also showed them we were willing to go the extra mile to provide something to these kids and their families that few people would do for free. It showed them that we should take whatever gifts and talents we possess and use those to share with others. It was also a bonus for them to see these kids and parents blown away and thankful for what ended up being a very small amount of time, effort and investment. Try doing a slideshow for a couple of family events first, before tackling a project like this so you don't get rushed by time constraints and deadlines.

73

Complete a high ropes course together

For those of us who have been to a camp in the mountains, high ropes courses are nothing new; for those of you who never seen one; they are a challenging way to encourage one another to do something they would never have dreamed of doing before. High ropes courses are typically a series of challenges involving climbing gear on your body; complete with safety rigging, climbing up different elements (with names like Jacob's Ladder, the Pamper Pole and the Rock Wall) and overcoming something. The elements are designed to be safe but to challenge one to overcome certain fears in order to complete the challenge. Certain fears that may be dealt with are heights, strength, and reliability on others.

Families can enjoy a morning or afternoon at a high ropes course and learn that much of what needs to be overcome in life (and at the high ropes course) can be done with enough encouragement. Many people don't realize how paralyzing it is to stand on top of a bare power pole 40 ft. up as it sways in the wind with the objective to jump to the trapeze handle 7 ft. away. With enough encouragement from others it can be done; and if you miss you rely on the person holding the belay rope, which is attached to your climbing harness so you won't fall to the ground

One of the highlights of our Family Camp we went to together was my son and I walking up the mountain, then up the tower and getting harnessed in to ride the ½ mile zip line together. I still remember my son's face as we started out and the apprehensive look he had in jumping off the tower. Within 5 seconds he was yelling with excitement as he zipped across the valley below; when we finished his first words were "Can we do it again Dad?!" High ropes courses offer something for everyone and even if someone is physically limited in completing any of the elements, they can still use their ability to encourage as others complete the challenges of the course.

74

Kidnap your children from school and go somewhere unexpected and fun

Okay, I'm not advocating keeping your kids from going to school, but if they are doing well, who is it going to hurt if they take one day off? If you are worried about the school getting their money, let them go for an hour and pick them up mid-morning so the school will still be reimbursed by the state. Spending a special day with your children when they know the alternative would be studying math or earth science is a great way to show your children you understand that schoolwork is hard, but once in awhile a break is okay.

I believe this also sends a message to our children that we as parents enjoy time with them; even time that we have to create. It says to our kids that we will go out of our way to plan and execute something special on their behalf. As I think about it, I believe it also shows our kids that although we value hard work and we want them to value hard work as well, we all need a little relief in our lives; even unexpected relief.

These kidnapped days are a great time to go to the beach or an amusement park when the crowds are down. It's also a good time to visit with older family members who don't get to see the children as much as they like to. Another possibility is to visit your spouse at their job with the children and kidnap them for lunch for a special unexpected meal together. The key is to make the time between you and them special and honoring.

75

Go to a pottery store and have each family member paint something for someone else in the family

We have a local store near my home that allows average people with no background in creating pottery art to go in and purchase a pottery item, paint it there and then leave it to be fired in their kiln for a shiny, glazed effect, which then the object can be picked up later when ready. The store has many different items from ceramic letters, pots to hold plants, ceramic animals, figurines, and jewelry boxes to vases; the selection is vast.

For families this is a special opportunity to create something special for another family member. This can be done with all family members present or done separately so each family member will be surprised when they receive their item.

This is a special time to create a memento that will stay with a family member their entire life (as long as it doesn't break). It will also form a memory in the life of the one who created the art piece that there is something special in creating an object of beauty for others that we care about.

This also opens up a door of creativity within children (and ourselves) that we have never experienced before. It shows us that we can create something that maybe we never thought we would have the ability to create before. Learning art with our children is a great way to express ourselves in a way that might not have an ability to be expressed previously. What's great about this idea is that you can start off small and inexpensive and work your way up to something larger and more costly the next time.

76

Cut down a Christmas tree together

Christmas decorating is a special time for most families. The lights, the smells, the presents, and the atmosphere; but the tree holds a special place for most families as well. Adorned with ornaments, lights, pictures, stringed popcorn or cranberries and the tree topper (which in our house is a crystal angel); these things make the tree a focal point in most family's homes leading up to Christmas day.

Picking out a tree is a special tradition as well. Noble or Douglas fir; 6 footer or 12 footer; tall and narrow or fat and round; flocked or natural? So many choices to consider. For families that choose to cut down their own tree at a Tree Lot that allows that; the decision becomes a little more personal because the one cutting the tree now has a special bond with the tree.

Choosing to cut down your own tree as a family allows the family to work together to fall a tree that will become a central figure in the family's celebration. It's a moment in a family's journey together that will forever be remembered as one of the special moments within the life of that family that will be relived every Christmas as your kids tell your grandkids what Christmas was like when they grew up.

77

Rent an RV and take a trip

My family has toyed with this idea and I think we are getting close. For many people who own RV's, going without one is almost unthinkable. RV's aren't cheap; the payment, the insurance, storage, the gas and the maintenance; these things keep many of us from ever experiencing what it feels like to hit the open road with our mobile house and our family together heading down the highway.

But taking a trip together in an RV does not have to be expensive. Families can rent an RV and pay for the gas for the trip cheaper then three months worth of payments, insurance and maintenance; without ever having to worry about storage or depreciation costs. Many RV rental centers exist and finding one is as simple as going to Google and typing in RV rental center and your location. Some RV rental centers will even bring the RV to your house and pick it up when you are finished. Driving one is as easy as driving a large van with just a little extra care needed when going around corners and into areas with low overhangs. Most RV rental centers can give you information on camping areas that have good facilities for families, but you can also find that information on the internet as well.

Like camping, RVing is a good way to spend time with your family while enjoying an adventure of something different. It also is one of those vacations that allow everyone to have a part in the responsibility. Unlike tent camping though, there is a little more security against the elements and local wild life and not as much setup needed to enjoy your camping trip. The added bonus of RVing is that families have an open room to enjoy during the drive; including a refrigerator and bathroom. Families can watch movies, play board or video games or sleep comfortably while parents are driving (seatbelt laws still are in effect for passengers in RVs).

78

Carve a pumpkin

Every Halloween season, it amazes me to see these pumpkin carvings that look more like works of art then decorations for the front porch. And the sad reality is that some kid is probably going to smash it before the night is over because I ran out of full-size candy bars. The last few years, my son and I have played around with making our pumpkins more artistic then just the standard Jack-O-Lantern face.

Patterns, cordless drills and dremel tools are part of the equation to achieve something beyond the normal scary, triangle-eyed, semi-toothless gourd head. My son and I also thought about putting our favorite baseball team logo on the pumpkin (Los Angeles Angels of Anaheim) but since the name change, we can't fit all the words on it.

Carving pumpkins, like any holiday tradition is something kids will hold close to their heart and look forward to each year. As they get into their teens they may drift away from the idea of helping, but they still want you to do it (this is where you allow them to begin to carve their own pumpkins). As they have their own family someday, they will carry on the tradition; especially if you built it up as something your family annually does.

79

Have a cookie-decorating contest

Kids love being creative and kids love cookies; decorating cookies is a natural fun event for most kids. Most families think about decorating cookies during the holiday season; but cookie decorating is a blast anytime during the year. Cookie decorating can be themed for certain holidays, seasons or special events like birthday celebrations.

Having a cookie-decorating contest in your family should be more about the fun of decorating cookies as it is about competition; although as kids get older they want to really compete. Thought should be given to the idea of creating enough rewards for each member of the family to receive one award a piece (such as most creative, closest to the theme, neatest, etc.); this takes away the idea of competing against one another and rewarding based on strength.

Cookie decorating becomes a bigger event when we as parents provide more utensils and decorations to make the decorated cookies even more spectacular; different cookie-cutter shapes, different frostings and frosting applicators, different colored sugars and sprinkles; even candy for adornments; these all add to the ability to create a cookie of majestic proportions.

80

Play HORSE

HORSE is a basketball game. It is a game that is played more for shooting and creative ability then it is dribbling and stamina ability. HORSE is a game that is played between two or more players and all that is needed is a basketball and a basketball hoop. Before the game begins, players all take a shot to see the order that each player will shoot; first player to sink a basket is the first player to go and so on until an order is established.

The first player to go takes his shot, if he makes it, the next player has to imitate that shot and make it; if he misses he gets the first letter in HORSE which is H. If he makes it, the next player has to shoot the same way, if he makes it, the next player goes and so on until it gets back to the original player that made the shot; he then gets to attempt a different shot. If any player misses, then the next player gets to attempt any shot of his choice. If he misses the next player gets to try to sink a bucket of his own creation until somebody makes it. If a player misses a shot that is being attempted for the first time, that player does not get a letter. Once a player gets all the letters in HORSE they are out of the game and players continue until all but one player is left. If you want to play a shorter game, you can play PIG or GOAT as well.

Games like this are fun for families in that they promote sports, family togetherness and fun that doesn't cost anything. It's also a great way to gauge your child's development as you see them progress in their athleticism and confidence. It's also a great time to encourage your children to try and up their game in an attempt to beat you as the parent; and when they do it's a great time to acknowledge their ability. Care must be taken as a parent not to get so into the game as to cause your child in becoming contemptuous against competing against you because your zealousness for wining overshadows the time spent with them.

81

Read your children bedtime stories

My wife and I heard one time before we ever had kids that if you want your child to be a good reader, then you must read to them often. My wife and I took that idea to heart and began reading to them as soon as they began to have the ability to listen and comprehend. In fact, our children's bookshelves are stuffed with books that we have read to them and with them over the short course of their lives; usually at night when we are attempting to get them to go to sleep.

For both of our children, this at times has not always been easy and sometimes we needed to bait the process in order to keep it going. Allowing our children to pick out their own books has been something that both of our children have enjoyed and we often find ourselves walking through the kid's area in the local bookstores helping them find that next story we will adventure through together.

For all of us, this has been a great experience. My kids talk fondly of these times and we know we haven't outgrown it yet when our kids still ask us to read to them. As mentioned above, we believe this has helped our kids strive toward becoming better readers. Both of our children are voracious readers and both of them have reading and comprehension levels multiple grades above their peers.

82

Go to a rescue mission and help serve the less fortunate

While watching the TV this last weekend, which was a holiday weekend, my son and I were reminded of how thoughtful and good people can be when they aired a piece about the local rescue mission and people coming to help serve a meal. I have served a ton of meals at local rescue missions and what I have experienced and what I have found over and over again is that doing this type of work, while benefiting to the people who are hungry; is mostly beneficial to our souls when we are serving. Something happens when one puts themselves in a servant position to those who are mostly broken and needy.

Taking your family to serve at a homeless or rescue mission is a great way to experience this soul-changing moment together. Watching your children and having your children watch you serve others is something amazing as well. Times like these are what defines a family's character and you will plot the course of goodwill in your children's hearts for the rest of their lives when you give in this charitable way. And although you will not be repaid in dollars or cents, you will be able to witness your family becoming more selfless in it's approach toward life and toward each other.

One thing to note about these opportunities is that they will not come and knock at your door. You must be proactive to find these opportunities. You have to be the one to call the local rescue mission, feeding ministry or shelter to ask if they need help. Calling at non-holiday times is usually appreciated because everyone calls to help at Thanksgiving or Christmas. Make sure to tell them you would like to bring your children because some missions and ministries are not set up for children and some of them have insurance regulations prohibiting children helping; but you won't know until you ask.

83

Go on a geo-caching adventure

If your family likes adventure and technology, this is the game for you. The website www.geocaching.com defines geocaching this way: "Geocaching is a high-tech treasure hunting game played throughout the world by adventure seekers equipped with GPS devices. The basic idea is to locate hidden containers, called geocaches, outdoors and then share your experiences online. Geocaching is enjoyed by people from all age groups, with a strong sense of community and support for the environment"; I couldn't have said it better myself.

Of the people I know who do this with their family, they seem to really enjoy the adventure of finding the treasure; sometimes you'll find something good, other times you'll find something not as good; but searching is half the fun. It's also a great way to get out and possibly explore an area you have never been to. The geocaching community seems to be a tight-knit group of people that utilize high-technology (GPS technology was only available for military applications less then 10 years ago) to have fun and to share that fun with others.

One of the great possibilities with geo-caching is that it is catching on all over the world. Whether you are going on vacation or visiting relatives, all one needs to bring is their GPS device and coordinates for the geocache to have some diverted fun. Little prizes seem to be the normal treasure one leaves as well as finds in the geocache containers, so make sure to bring something to leave; possibly something familiar to the area where you live.

84

Fix up your child's car together

There might be a little bit of time before you really need to do this; but what would stop someone from doing this now; if the benefit was time between you and your child. Some kids enjoy books, some kids enjoy computers, and some enjoy wrenching on a 69 Mustang Fastback with their dad (and maybe mom).

Unless one is loaded with a ton of money, fixing up a car is never cheap, easy or quick. If your child is 8 or 9, I would think it is a perfect time to look around for a fixer upper that you and your child can begin to pour time, money, blood, sweat and tears into preparing it for that day he/she will drive it to school or the mall when they are 16.

Besides time with their parents, fixing up a car together over a longer period of time also gives a child a sense of ownership that they won't be as apt to abuse when they do start to drive. It also gives parents an opportunity now to challenge their children toward keeping grades up and being a responsible person through dialoguing about what they are working toward and the rewards of working diligently. When you give yourself time to work on a car, you also know there is no rush to buy at any certain time; look around and wait for the good deal.

85

Go to a food fair or community taste event

Community food fairs or taste events are a great way to experience local restaurant's food without having to commit to visiting the restaurant. It also a great way to gauge whether their food is going to be kid-friendly or within the taste parameters that your family has already established.

Community food fairs and taste events exist to show off these restaurants in order to increase customer traffic into their establishments. Often times there is also music and other non-food related performances occurring at the events as well. Many of these events have kid-zones for your children to enjoy themselves for a while as well. Most of these events have an at-the-door cost and script is purchased inside to use to purchase plates of food and drinks.

Having been to quite a few of these, the best time for families is during the day. This is when the crowds are lowest and food portions are typically larger. Most kid-type activities happen during the day as well. Since these events are usually held outside, they are mostly summertime events; so dressing your kids appropriately for comfort and sun-protection is going to be a must.

86

Watch movies outside as a family

Growing up, one of the fun family things we did do together was going to the drive-in movies. Always a double-feature, always a playground to hit during the intermission; drive-ins were a blast when I was a kid. Unfortunately, drive-ins have mostly gone by the wayside and have pretty well vanished from the landscape (although a few still exist, they are definitely tougher to find these days then in the past). Families wanting to continue the thrill of a drive-in have now got to be creative in order to replicate that outdoor movie experience.

The beauty is that with video projection units becoming more and more popular and lower priced, families can enjoy that outdoor movie experience once again. Just like TVs, video projection units hook up to cable, VHS, DVD players and also DVR's like Tivo. All a family needs to enjoy a movie outside is a screen area to show the movie on which could be as simple as a bed sheet or a blank wall or as sophisticated as an inflatable outdoor screen which is marketed for just such a purpose as this (checkout ww.backyardtheater.com for some cool ideas).

The great thing about watching movies outside with your family is the fact that it is a novel idea, so there is excitement built in and also there is the cuddling factor. When out side, families usually sit real close to keep warm; so the cuddling factor becomes a bonus for families when watching movies outside. It's also a great idea to invite neighbors to; set up an outside microwave and have them bring their own popcorn. Don't forget: whoppers mixed with popcorn is an incredible movie snack.

87

Make home made hot cocoa

In this day and age of pre-measured packets of hot cocoa, making homemade cocoa from scratch (homemade) is a concept many people unfortunately have a hard time wrapping their brain around. The truth is that hot cocoa hasn't always come from a pre-measured packet that comes out of a box of 10 or 20; there are actual recipes for hot cocoa that are very good and actually taste better then the packets (even the ones with the freeze-dried marshmallows).

The great thing about hot cocoa is that most kids love it; whether it is from a packet or from scratch. The bonus is that kids love to help and actually like something more when they have the opportunity to help prepare it. When a child is given the blessing of being able to help cook something they become attached a little easier to that item; especially if they are used to hot cocoa from a packet.

Recipes for hot cocoa can be found in most thorough cookbooks or look on the internet where recipes are very easy to find. Cocoa is relatively easy to make with the basic ingredients being cocoa, sugar, milk, vanilla, whip cream and marshmallows. Care must be given when allowing children to work around the stove; never allow a child to stir something that is higher then their chest; stand them on a step ladder or chair and always supervise. For added flair, shave pieces of chocolate bars onto the top of the whip cream.

88

Go horseback riding

With the industrialization and urbanization of most of America, horseback riding is not something most Americans have the opportunity to enjoy. And yet, horseback riding is still a draw for many families who desire to share with their children the beauty and power that horses display and the fun that can be accomplished with something that does not take a remote to operate.

Horseback riding is one of those pursuits that have a smell, feel and draw that is quite unique. The smell of the horse itself, the open air, the grass and trees or the area you are riding in, the leather smell of the saddle, the feel of the bridle, your body in the saddle, your feet in the stirrups, boots, the rush of a horse at full gallop; these are the attractions your family will experience when you take them horseback riding.

Many families are reluctant to take their family riding because of the possible accidents that could occur on the back of such a powerful animal. Most family riding stables have horses that are family friendly and the threat of an accident has been minimized as much as possible with docile animals and easy riding trails. Family friendly costs are also a plus as most stables are looking to get more families involved in riding and horse ownership.

89

Sew a family quilt together

Okay, I'm a guy and I don't sew. But truth be told: I see a nice handcrafted quilt and I admire the workmanship (workwoman-ship?) that has gone into that piece. As a craftsman myself, I also admire the talent that it took to create that piece, knowing it took time and practice to make such a piece so beautiful. Quilting is one of those hobbies/trades that have been around before Spanish and European travelers ever made it to the Americas. Although quilting spurs on images of little old ladies sitting around a table sewing and gossiping; quilting is serious business to many (many of which are men).

Putting a family quilt together is a family project that will take some encouraging to get everyone to participate. The great thing about making a quilt is that everyone can be involved. From picking out the pattern, to cutting the fabric pieces and internal batting, to stitching and sewing; everybody can participate. This is a great project that also can show family members how to do basic sewing in case they need to hem a pair of pants or sew a patch onto the sleeve of their baseball or soccer jersey.

Deciding what type of quilt to create is probably the part which generates the most energy in this project; each family member needs to be represented. Some families are creating family quilts, which utilize digital photography and the ability to print pictures and text from ink jet and laser printers onto fabric. This could also be a project where the family crest is emblazoned on the front of the quilt (check out that previous section on family crests). Whatever you choose to create, make sure to keep in mind you'll need to make one for each of your children because items like these will be fought over when your huge estate is someday divided!

90

Go to an air-show

Living less then a mile from a public airport and within a 2-hour drive of three military bases; air shows are a part of life in this area of California. Air shows are a great way for private owners to show off their skills and planes and for the military to showcase their deadly hardware and their best pilots operating them.

Air shows can be a great day for families to spend time together looking at and talking about the differing types of aircraft that are on display (both in the air and on the ground). Standing next to a stealth bomber, guarded by security with M-16s, children and adults are equally mesmerized by the intensity of such an expensive and powerful machine. This feeling is repeated throughout the day as attendees view the vintage aircraft, support aircraft, helicopters and the fighter jets.

But aside from seeing the aircraft perform amazing acrobatic stunts and death-defying routines; air shows are a great way to spend time together. With a fair-like atmosphere, air shows are a mixture of circus, high technology, showmanship and food; there is always something to watch and there is always some new food to try. Air shows give us an opportunity to dialogue with our kids about dreaming big dreams and what it takes to become a pilot and the many hours of studying and training to achieve their dream of someday flying; this discussion with your children can be transferred into many discussions about many career options in their lives. If you haven't been to an airshow before, be prepared to bring in chairs, blankets, and possibly a cooler (if allowed) to have snacks throughout the day for your kids.

91

Go whale watching

Few things in life can compare to the image of a blue whale, gray whale or killer whale coming to the surface, close enough that you could reach your hand out and touch it's head or pet it's back fin. Whale watching is one of those opportunities you can do with your family that allows you to enjoy different facets of nature; from the coastline to the ocean to the sea life that you will see on your trip.

Okay, truth be told; this will be pretty tough if you live in Wisconsin; but maybe a vacation is in order; I wouldn't necessarily plan a vacation around whale watching, but it certainly is worth including if you were going to be in the area during the migration period. Whales migrate in both the Pacific and Atlantic oceans. You could check the internet for contact information and pricing of whale watching tours that will be departing near the area you might be vacationing.

You might also make sure to bring sunblock, Dramamine for motion sickness and jackets because it can get cooler once you get out on the water; kids will feel the exposure more because their skin is thinner.

92

Build a sand castle

Kids of all ages love building sand castles; especially when adults help to make the castle as authentic as possible. Kids love the imagination that goes into putting a sand castle together, the thought of what it could be vs. what actually gets built; the different parts of the castle and what purpose they serve. The dugout moat and water rushing in to fill it to keep all the bad knights and evil villains out; kids can have a blast working with sand because it can take on a life all it's own.

Whatever theirs (or yours) technical skill or background, understanding of architecture (most of them don't have any) sandcastles always become a short-lived work of art that produces hours of entertainment; mostly fueled by imagination. We as the adults have the responsibility to fuel this imaginative building project by providing the essentials to complete such a great project.

Buckets are always a staple, shovels (hand shovels work well and aren't as dangerous); spray bottle to keep sand moderately moist, small containers of differing shapes, flags mounted on sticks; even plastic little knights or army men can make the sand castle more interesting. The key is to enjoy your time together. Don't get to wrapped up in the perfection of the building, but immerse yourself in the time spent with your children having fun creating something that will be gone soon with the changing of the tide.

93

Watch planes take off and land

There is something magical about watching a plane take off and land; especially a large jet. When given the opportunity to sit and watch planes do this from a vantage point that is close enough that one can feel the rumble of the jets as they pass; it's almost surreal; unless of course you're a pilot or work at an airport; then it's normal everyday stuff. For most of us and our kids, this is a special time to talk about what it takes to fly, where someone can fly to and why it's so expensive to fly.

My family would sometimes go over to John Wayne Airport in Orange County to do this. We would park in a parking lot next to the airport but adjacent to the runway to watch the planes as they came and went. It was interesting to note that we would be dialoguing with each other but when the plane was on approach or getting ready to take off, we were all silent, watching in anticipation for the touchdown or the takeoff. We would talk about the different carriers and where they mostly flew to; we would talk about how they keep the planes safe in the air and we would talk about how fast they are going and how much runway it took to stop such a big plane.

This was a great place to talk with our kids and share with them some of the stories of traveling that their mother and I have experienced. It gave us a chance to share about some of the scary moments of traveling and also some of the better and funnier moments. It was a time to begin talking about future trips we wanted to take as a family and where someday our kids wanted to travel on their own. Watching planes take off and land for our family was about taking some time to discuss the world of travel with our kids.

94

Play Bocce together

I never played Bocce until I met my wife's family. Being of Italian descent, my wife's family would play Bocce at family picnics; of which they had many. What I found out about Bocce is that you don't have to be of Italian ancestry or be in great shape to have fun and actually compete in the sport of Bocce.

Bocce is a docile game played between individuals or between teams. Most Bocce sets come with two colored groups of balls (usually made of wood, very heavy, about 4 inches in diameter) and a small ball called a jack or a boccino. One player will throw the jack in a certain direction and then teams take turns throwing the Bocce balls toward the jack to attempt to get their teams Bocce balls closest to the jack. Points are awarded to the two closest balls to the jack. Games are typically played to 11, 12 or 13. In official games, play is conducted within a certain bounded area; in our family games, we would utilize the entire grassy area of the park (small rolling hills included).

Bocce is a great way to spend an afternoon with your family. Whether athletic or not, Bocce is fun for all that play. Bocce is more about strategy then it is about athleticism and people of all ages can have a great time playing.

95

Go play miniature (putt-putt) golf

I'm not a golfer, but I honestly believe if there were a pro tour circuit for miniature golf; I could be on it, and I could win big prize money. Miniature golf (or putt-putt golf as it is known in some places) is one of those rare activities that you really need no true skill in to have fun and actually do well in. Windmills, water hazards and multi-level hole shots are just some of the reasons and challenges that make mini-golf a great time.

But I think what makes mini-golf fun for kids is that it is a mini-scale version of a multi-sensory fantasy land that has challenges to overcome before they can see or experience the remainder of the course. Kids love engaging in a challenge where they don't know what is coming up, but they know it's going to be exciting. It's also a place where kids need to be taught how to "tap" or "putt" the ball properly to keep it on the course; these lessons come from parents. This experience becomes a lesson in self-control; self control for the child in not hitting the ball as hard as possible and in the parents to not get upset that their child can't hit the ball properly and to stay and continue playing the game. Mini golf is a great time of having silly, controlled fun with no real objective other then having fun hanging out with one another. By the way: if you are taking your kids to play mini golf just to show them your advanced skills on the putting green and you are going to keep score to make sure they know who the champion is in the family; then at least play them left-handed (unless you already are left-handed) to give them a fighting chance to rub it in your face once in awhile.

Another nice thing about mini golf is that it is relatively inexpensive. A family of four can usually play for about the same cost as matinee tickets at a local movie theater; without the cost of popcorn, candy and sodas. Beware though; the arcade can get pricey afterwards. My son and I will usually play a couple of games of Time Crisis 3 in the arcade to round off our time together.

96

Have the "talk" with your kids before they are too old

Let's clarify something that most parents already understand: when I say the "talk", I am talking about the "sex talk"; one of the scarier moments of being a parent. So scary, that many parents choose to avoid the talk altogether and allow society (mostly media and friends) to dictate how your child feels and understand about their own sexuality; parents stepping in only when their child gets in troubling spots or gets hurt doing something they shouldn't have been involved with. Because this is such an important issue, entire books have been written on the subject; I cannot do it the justice it needs in three paragraphs, but I can encourage you to consider how important it is to have this talk and to plan on having it at some point when it is age appropriate; not waiting until your child is already tainted with other information about the subject.

This being said, unless you live in a bubble, your child by the age of 8 is already being bombarded with images and messages concerning this area. This may not manifest itself in any manner through the next few years but by the time they begin their steps into adolescent development; they will already have the information necessary to put two and two together and form

181

their own conclusions; which is already becoming too late; which makes this "talk" more necessary early rather then later. Contrary to what many parents think or feel; having the talk with your child about sex and sexuality will not give them license to go out and hook up with somebody of the opposite sex. In fact, most of the time it will take away the curiosity of the act and give them understanding that there are repercussions if they choose to engage early rather then waiting for marriage.

As mentioned earlier, there are great books written on this subject that I would have no problem recommending.

97

Without meddling, keep informed of your child's relationships

What we've learned with our two children is that they were forming and managing relationships with others long before they started school. Neighbors, playgrounds and Church all opened up our children's world to the possibility of forming relationships. Not just friends of the same sex, but friends of the opposite sex as well. They were recognizing what their similarities and what their differences were. They formed opinions (some on their own, some because of their peers) and they came to conclusions about others; some of these conclusions were justified ("Brandon's a bully because he pulled all the girls hair; Sophia is nice because she shared her cupcake with me, etc.), and some of them were unjustified because of biased presuppositions. But as our kids shared these insights, we saw our kids past the routine parental viewpoint that we had possessed over the last few years of their life and we began to see into a window of how our kids were really shaped.

As our kids shared about these peer relationships we always kept an open discussion policy; encouraging our kids to share what they thought and what they observed without making judgments or closed-ended statements that would cause them to stop sharing with us. This allowed an ongoing dialogue between us that helped us to support and encourage them in relationship building and making. Having this type of approach of being interested in our child's relationships without attempting to over-manage those relationships, we found our kids less apt to hold back things they didn't want us to know for fear of reprisal or backlash.

This also allowed us to know which friends were influencing our kids and how best to work them around problems associated with those kids and the possible negativity that could be a result of that relationship. Most kids hold their friends in high value (sometimes more so than their own family) so it's important to find ways to influence your child in a positive direction when friends might be doing the opposite. We've learned an informed but loose hold on these relationships without judgment keeps the doorway open for knowing who is influencing our children and gives us the ability to make suggestions without condemnation from them. The exception to this obviously is when we find out our child is being harmed or in potential harm, then we have stepped in with full force and dealt with things as the situation has necessitated correcting the situation.

98

Hug and kiss your children; often.

Both medical and psychological studies have concluded that children need positive physical touch in their various development stages to be healthy; both physically and psychologically. Kids need these hugs and kisses because it helps them to know that they can feel good enough about themselves that people that are close to them are not afraid to touch them in healthy ways. This is very important in the immediate family, because we see each other at our best and worst and physical touch is a salve to soothe any wounds that might get inflicted by omission or by commission. In our society (and in my own family) we make jokes about the grandma or aunt who wants to give the big wet kiss and also a bear hug and how kids hate it; and yet kids will talk about that grandma or aunt and their wet kisses the rest of their lives.

Both of my children have been raised on a steady diet of healthy physical touch. We kiss, we hug, we wrestle, we hold hands and we scratch each other's backs; why? Because healthy physical touch is necessary to have healthy self-esteems, healthy understandings of boundaries and healthy understandings about appropriate touch. We believe these things are necessary in our child's development to create adults someday that will have a healthy understanding of themselves and of what it takes to have healthy relationships with others.

This is not to say we don't realize there will be limitations on these things as they get older. I joke with my son, who is 8 now whether or not he will still kiss me when he is in high school; he says he will, but that will remain to be seen. My daughter (who is older then her brother) and I still have a great relationship and we have many moments where she hugs me or gives me a kiss; but not in front of her friends.

99

When away, call your kids

Because of the nature of the work I do, traveling is not an option. Camps, mission trips, conferences and speaking opportunities; as much as I enjoy these things, they do take me away from my family and it does cause me to miss them and for them to miss me as well. With the exception of traveling with my entire family, getting around this problem is not possible, but some of the problems associated with traveling and the stress and heartache it causes on my family has been reduced by attempting to keep in contact as much as possible; preferably by phone.

I say phone because there is something soothing about each other's voice that can't be replaced by email, text messaging or postcards. When I travel I expect to use my phone to stay in contact with my family even if that means paying outrageous fees to do so. With my cell phone and an international calling plan, I can usually get in touch with my family within a few seconds of calling; and vice versa. I've also learned when in another country to buy a calling card (usually off a street vendor) and pay for calls this way. This saves me about 75% of the fee it would be if I used my own carrier and plan to take care of the call. This may be negotiated with your employer to be included in necessary expenses for the trip as well.

The stress and heartache that I mentioned above should not be underestimated either. A parent that travels regularly adds a level of stress to a child's life (and spouse) that somehow needs to be minimized. This doesn't just have to do with the threat of your means of traveling but also the thought of you not being there when they sleep at night or being home for dinner. Your calling home regularly or allowing your children to call you once per day adds a great deal of relief to their minds as they deal with you being away. It may infringe somewhat on your personal finances, but it will do much for keeping your relationship with your family healthy.

100

Model random acts of kindness for others

If you didn't already know this, your kids learn much of what they know by what they've seen you do. Their views on life, their thoughts on others, how they act in certain situations, and various presuppositions are all mostly a result of what they have seen and heard in their parents. Parents are the number one shaping force in a child's life, nothing in this world carries with it the responsibility and influence that a parent does; which makes the job of parenting a huge burden to bear that should not be taken lightly. As a parent, know that your kids are watching you. And what they see will make a huge impact on their own lives.

And how you live your life should be important to us as parents. Do you want your child to be a person of compassion and service or do you as a parent want your child to be selfish and greedy in how they approach others? Most of us would say we want our kids to be compassionate and giving, ready to help others when situations dictate such. This, I believe does not come naturally, it is a learned behavior. They learn first by seeing us doing. If a child sees us walking by a person in need or ignoring those who are down on their luck in life, they will learn to do the same. On the contrary, if they see us as people who are helping others when it is needed; they too will be more apt to help.

And the attitude needs to go beyond just people we know and toward helping others regardless of our affiliation with them. If you wonder if your helping a homeless person in front of your children matters, understand that it does. If you wonder whether your choosing an Angel from a Project Angel Tree stand at the mall to purchase a gift for the child of an incarcerated mom or dad matters; understand it does. As parents, we need to be the first ones to model random acts of kindness, because it makes a huge and positive impact on the lives and thoughts of our children. Want your children to be selfless, helpful, charitable and giving toward others, be the first to model it for them and they will.